BORN IN SIN,
UPENDED IN GRACE

a memoir

For Anne & Tom

In appreciation for your
critical reviews of the book,
Tom's endorsement, and a
deeply valued friendship.

Love,
George

BORN IN SIN, UPENDED IN GRACE

a memoir

George Williamson

*Published by
the Baptist Peace Fellowship of North America
Bautistas por la Paz*

For Carol

*Beloved and necessary
companion on this adventure,
my fiercest defender,
who's appalled at about
half my shenanigans,*

*and for the late Mac Bryan,
mentor,*

*and the late Cliff Hendrix,
co-conspirator.*

ISBN 978-0-9622896-5-1

First Printing in 2016
by the Baptist Peace Fellowship of North America
Bautistas por la Paz
All Rights Reserved
Typeset in Cambria with Trajan Pro titles
designed by Double Vision Press

ACKNOWLEDGMENTS

This memoir would never have seen the light of day had it not been for the generous decision by the Board of the Baptist Peace Fellowship of North America/Bautistas por la Paz, and especially its Communications Committee, to publish it. We are especially indebted to LeDayne McLeese Polaski for proposing this project and shepherding its completion. My friend Claudia Esslinger readily agreed to do the design and get our friend, Julie Reiswig, to help her wrench it into editorial shape, and Allison Paksoy has bravely drug it through the thicket of publication details.

I've received crucial guidance through the secrets of the literary world by my agent, Ed Breslin. Joyce Starr did critical editorial revisions. Encouragement and critical feedback has kept me going and dragged me back on course time and again; from, Betsy and John Lane, Anne Barstow, Tom Driver, Cheryl Dudley, Adam Phillips, David Schalk, David Robb, Jim Phillips, Bob Fortna, and especially my discerning and enormously caring kids, Peter, Dan, and Chris, and their endlessly supportive and mercilessly critical mother, my wife, Carol.

My teachers, my colleagues through the years, my close friends, my wider family, including the Wagster clan—a huge gift of great grace given me by Carol—my faculty companions at Vassar College and the incredible students that institution entrusted to me, the people of First Baptist, now, First United Church, of Granville, and for thirty years, everyone at the Baptist Peace Fellowship: all of these have nourished and empowered me, and given me more or less everything I know and have.

To all these, this memoir, such as it is, is your tribute.

George Williamson
New York City
November 1, 2015

CONTENTS

Introduction

Contents, cont.

INTRODUCTION

My journey has been a convoluted pilgrimage through a rapid succession of moral social movements that played out in my little life. I was born on the wrong side of them all, a true believer in everything elitist, sexist, homophobic, profligate, anti-Semitic, and Jim Crow.

I grew up in postwar Atlanta, specifically Buckhead, the privileged northern quarter. I was above average in the things that made my parents proud: church, school work, politeness. I parted my hair most mornings, zipped up my pants, said "Hi" a lot. But I was way below average in sports and social cool. I attended college at a Baptist school due to the above and because they didn't allow dancing on campus. I evolved into a career more marked by dismissals, ejections, and controversy than by the trophies of achievement. I was an unremarkable husband, father, and grandfather, though in a remarkable family.

But this story is not about what I did. Life happens while we try to make sense and sensible choices. Not that we're condemned to the passive voice. I'm certainly not. Life is chaotic, untold. Making sense of it, telling and taking up the tale is fatefully active, but I've heard in intimate detail the circumstances of many others. If what happened to them had happened to me (instead of what did), I would not be recognizable as me. Life happens to you.

What befell me were the signature social movements that made sport of those years, each of which, as we slanged in Buckhead, turned me every way but loose. Starting out on the wrong side, I got blindsided by one after another of them, upended and catapulted, suddenly and often traumatically, to the notorious front end of the other side. I was a church boy, standing literally on my head, rooted in the nourishing soil of the wrong side, now suddenly uprooted and toppled onto my feet.

The story has theological significance, a somewhat comic collision of Sin and Grace, two notorious theological words. However, as secular readers will quickly discover, theological does not mean Religious Dogma and does not mean the Dogmas which make up Religion. I haven't much truck with Dogma or Religion. Theology is a word having to do with God, the ineffable source of all things and guarantor of Love. It's not something I believe or don't believe in. God is beyond belief, worship, and things religious. God, as I engage God, is simply the foundation of everything I care about.

In truth, what I do is less theology and more homiletics. Homiletics is a seminary word that means preaching. Whatever I may be, I'm a preacher. Theologians are obliged to figure it out and make it consistent. Preachers are in the trenches, having to come out with it week after every week, obliged to make it plain and move on.

This book is written for seekers and pilgrims fascinated or perhaps confused by the social revolutions of our time. It's meant for those who would be upended by Grace, and for readers still standing on their heads over choices yet to be made. It's also intended to be enjoyed, just as the living of it has been enjoyed. My life has been infused with far more than my share of joy.

I do not claim that what happened to me is unique, quite the opposite. It happened, more or less, to us all.

MARTIN LUTHER KING, JR.

I made the journey across the colossal existential chasm of seeming infinite depth, from Buckhead to Sweet Auburn and Ebenezer Church. I stepped through the door, imagining myself to be the first white guy ever to do so, was greeted by the white toothy smile and white boutonnière of a very black usher in still blacker duds, and was guided to the front row past the turning heads of women in astonishingly colorful hats.

I was relieved to see that the preacher was Dr. Martin Luther King, but surprised that there was also a Dr. Martin Luther King, "Jr." on the program and a "Mrs. Martin Luther King" at the organ.

I was confused. The Martin Luther King, rabble-rouser on television and in the newspaper photos was young. He couldn't possibly have a son who was a "Dr." The woman at the organ seemed much older. When she cranked up the pipes, two robed preachers strode to the platform: the TV rabble-rouser and a powerfully built older gentleman.

The elder King preached the sermon, a rip-snorting stem winder. It was about Joshua and the tumbling wall of Jericho. Blocking entrance to the Promised Land against a people called there by God, the walls were meant to keep "the enemy out," he declared. Yet they actually prevented "the enemy within" from entering the Promised Land. Walls may repel armies, the elder King cried with flourish, but are powerless before the spiritual power of inspired people, and the "trumpet blast" of a prophet at their head. I thought he was preaching to me, just me. I felt a "wall" in the vicinity of my beating heart come tumbling down—like the night at Ridgecrest when I gave up dancing, for God. Tears blotted my cheeks, and when he gave the Invitation to Come Forward, Accept Jesus and Join the Church, I tripped over myself to get up there and do it.

The rabble-rouser was indeed Dr. King, Jr. As fate would have it, Dr. King and his wife, Coretta (who wasn't the organist) invited me home for lunch, surrounded by their giggling children. I told them about growing up Jim Crow, stumbling into a Sit-in, getting arrested and having my world wrenched around. I said I didn't know who I was or what was happening, but I wanted to find out and be part of it.

Dr. King suggested that I work with him at the Southern Christian Leadership Conference the following summer, and I did. I learned about Gandhi, social change, biblical justice, and radical political strategy, and I became the most famous white in the Civil Rights Movement.

Of course, none of this happened. It couldn't possibly have happened. It's a lifelong fantasy in which I've indulged myself, about how different life might have been were I not born in Sin. This book is, rather, about how it was.

BORN BORN AGAIN

I was Born in Sin. As I understood it, sin was a wanton want of being nice. This I learned at Second-Ponce de Leon Baptist Church in Buckhead, Georgia, but it didn't matter, because I was also born Born Again, forty years before evangelical Republicans made Born Again a political shibboleth.

I knew I was born Born Again, because from birth I wanted to be a Baptist preacher. It was also because I was born at the center of the front row at church, squarely beneath Dr. Swilley's pulpit and the Tiffany chandelier in our big sanctuary. Not really the front row. The "Deacon's Bench" was the front row. It was reserved for people to be saved during the last hymn, weeping confession to the Deacon and signing up for life.

In truth, I was not really born on the front row or at the exact center. Hilda Hubbard was. Hilda was the star Christian in our class. Still is, circling the world for Jesus, risking her life in Afghanistan, tutoring Muslim women who risk their lives being tutored. She beat me at that and everything. I was reduced to sitting next to her three Sundays out of four, chin on fists atop the Deacon's Bench, eyes upturned to Dr. Swilley.

I also knew I was born Born Again because when I turned eight (old enough to be baptized) I realized I was Born Again already. I couldn't work up the general wretchedness I was supposed to feel for being Born in Sin, so as a strapping eight-year-old, I went forward one row at the end of worship, said the words to the Deacon, was baptized and got it over with. Nonetheless, from birth back in Nashville, Tennessee, I was on a descent into the notorious moral and spiritual malignancies of the age. Before I reached the front row at Second-Ponce de Leon, three fateful events occurred: We hired Nancy to look after me and wait on my parents; Herman Lay moved to Atlanta; and Uncle Popo went to war.

When I was born in Nashville, my parents put my crib in the hall closet of our little inner-city apartment, three blocks from what would be called Music Row. They hired a teenage "Negress," Nancy, so my mother, a twenty-eight-year-old, lower-middle-class white woman, could have full time "help." I don't remember much from my first three years, except for Nancy. She was beautiful, and with what little relevant plumbing I had to offer, I was in love.

Herman and Mimi Lay were church friends of my parents. Herman's tiny potato chip distributorship was across the street from our apartment. When the Atlanta company whose chips he sold went bankrupt, Herman borrowed a hundred dollars on his Model A Ford, a thousand on his distributorship, and got four thousand in investments from three men: the gas station owner next door, his insurance agent and the banker who loaned him thirty thousand more. With thirty-five thousand he bought the company. That and his move to Atlanta would prove fateful for the underbelly of my life.

Then my favorite Uncle Popo joined the Army. When his unit took charge of the Burma Road in India, my prayers were for Popo in battle, and for victory—my earliest spirituality. I would one day read Mark Twain's "The War Prayer"; his bitterly eloquent satire, in which prayer is not for our troops and victory, but for the implications: the other side's blasted hopes, slaughtered youth, their families' ruinous grief—in other words, my prayer. Childhood treasures include a photo of Captain Popo, heroic-looking in resplendent dress uniform, me on his lap, his cap askew on my head, military bravado inflaming my three-year-old features.

Wartime terrors crept out of my dark closet at night. In my forties I discovered *Faces of the Enemy,* by Sam Keen, a collection of cartoon distortions of "Krauts"and "Japs," the very faces from the closet. Having German and Japanese friends as an adult confronted me with the prejudices that shaped the contours of my young mind.

After Herman Lay moved to Atlanta, he persuaded Daddy to abandon his accounting career at National Life and Accident Insurance, where he wrote paychecks for WSM, the company's radio station, and the stars of its flagship "Grand Ole Opry" (Roy

Acuff, Hank Williams, Lefty Frizell). Daddy became Treasurer of H.W. Lay & Company, a title he still held at retirement, though the company had morphed into PepsiCo, with Herman as Chair of the Board. There began my descent into the moral and spiritual ambiguities of American Capitalism.

We brought Nancy, now our "live-in," to the green lawns of Buckhead, Atlanta's northern quarter. Renting a small house, we made part of the dirt basement, where coal was dumped, into a living space for Nancy. My mother exhibited a domestic genius, something I came to admire in my dotage. But since my earliest memory was of Daddy hiring a "maid" to help her, I felt deep condescension that domesticity, women's work, was something "even a Negress" could do.

It was 1942. I was three. Nightly, I fell asleep inchoately conscious that the pretty black girl who nourished me was trapped beneath my room in a fetid space I was afraid to enter, a dreadful image that symbolized my condition. One day Nancy disappeared, "ran away," my mother said in a panic, echoing the days of slavery. My three-year-old self was heartbroken... and relieved.

Later we moved to a house with a half-concrete basement. Our new basement had an electric light bulb, washing machine, double sink, washboard, hand-turned wringer and ironing board. There we hired Bessie, who came on the bus and didn't live in the basement. Still, she worked under the light bulb, next to the dirt, extending the vague sense that a grotesque substratum to my little house, my life, was under-girded by something dark.

By contrast was Eddie, head janitor at church. His balding brown pate trimmed with silver, Eddie was a sweet man with kind eyes and soft voice that floated a warm "George!" my way in greeting. He wore the white coat of a head servant. One of the reasons I so liked church is because its underpinnings, jolly and benign, were clad in white.

Forty years later, Rev. Emory Searcy, executive director of a prominent justice organization, joined a board I chaired. Discovering we were fellow Atlantans, he asked where I went to church. "My Sunday School teacher was head janitor there," he exclaimed, "the most prestigious job of anybody in my church. Mr. Mims was a great man, a powerful influence on my life. Did you know him?" I did, but when I knew him, fifty years my senior, he was just Eddie the janitor.

My parents were good people, as good as any I've ever known. They were extraordinarily attentive, affectionate and generous to me. Their only child, I felt the center of their lives. Daddy, whose name I carry, a gentle man and gentleman, the conscience of his company, was a leader at church. Son of grim Methodist moralists, he was renowned as a nonjudgmental teetotaler who enjoyed business and social relationships in which liquor flowed freely—except to him. He bore his parents' iron-core principles, but graciously. These included fair and truthful business dealings, unfailing kindness and lavish generosity. Politics he inherited from East Tennessee Republicans, an island of GOP since Lincoln, amid a Dixiecrat region where Democratic primaries counted as elections. He was conservative in all things. Only after I became a professional ethicist did it occur to me that his powerful principles applied only in the personal realm. He treated the social, political and economic order as simply amoral. I wanted to be like him— exactly.

We were pals, though in retrospect I recognize a want of intimacy. He died when I was thirty-five, before I learned much about his history or inner life. We rarely played ball but went to Atlanta Crackers games, followed them on radio and in the paper, and tracked their stars (especially Eddie Matthews) through major league careers. We obsessed together about the Georgia Tech Yellow Jackets, went to games, and on Sunday after church watched Coach Bobby Dodd analyze the previous day's game film.

We listened to recordings of Fred Waring and the Pennsylvanians, and after Sunday night church, as I sprawled center floor with my big bowl of oatmeal and mug of hot chocolate, we laughed with Milton Berle on TV. Daddy delighted in me, loved his work, was proud of his company, believed in his church, grew passionate weekly about "them Jackets!" and wept at the

Pennsylvanians' rendition of "The Battle Hymn of the Republic"—as I do still. For the most part, though, he betrayed little emotion.

My mother was called "Peggy" in the various circles through which she swirled, "Maggie Martin" by the mother who named her, and "Miss Peggy" by generations of Sunday School four-year-olds. She was "Kitty" to me, because that's what, on becoming verbal, I called her. She was tiny, graceful, soft—like a kitty—and embraced me in an oedipal bond that crowded dangerously to romantic. She was a joyous fairy of a woman and was popular her entire life. She was also the first I knew to possess a quality I would eventually devote myself to comprehending—CHARISMA.

We were indeed intimate—too intimate for the long-term health of our relationship. We spent hours at the kitchen table (the invisible "help" bustling invisibly around us) hashing through the day, wringing its remotest juices of gossipy thrill. Rare was the day Kitty didn't cry, despite the fact that she claimed, shaking off and denying her tears, to be "the happiest person alive." Much of what we talked about was me, my allegedly exceptional qualities by comparison to other kids.

She taught me that I, even more than she, was the happiest person alive. This was a mysterious truth she ground into me whenever I, though much less frequently than she, cried. Uncharacteristically she would make fun of my tears, shame me for them, underscore how fortunate I was, how little I had to cry about. And I was ashamed. And I learned not to cry or ever acknowledge a single negative in my sprawling little life.

Kitty and I talked frankly about Daddy whom we equally adored and admired. Daddy's stoicism was the example she'd always point to when scolding me for crying, but we'd regularly admit that neither had enough emotive metabolism with Daddy. And we regularly confessed, through Kitty's tears, how much we found in each other. She'd convince me to finish my meals with the old parental saw: "But what about the starving Armenian children?" Did my guilt-ridden ingestion feed a single Armenian—who can say?

We never—ever—talked about race, even after I stumbled

infamously, at twenty, into the politics of race. That's what I learned from both of them: not to talk about it. Kitty had a way of making light of what she disapproved with infectious laughter. It was an aspect of her charisma, part of what made her fun to be around.

Daddy showed his disapproval with a weary sigh, or more seriously, an uncharacteristic, therefore striking, grimace of disgust. This was a major component of his presence as a deeply moral man, his version of prophetic indignation—what I, along with many others, so admired about him. My parents' relations with black people seemed characteristically kind and generous, but something else—what I later learned to name "condescending."

Although I do not recall that my parents ever said a negative word, I observed that people of dark complexion were beneath them, and certainly beneath me; that they could not be communicated with in ordinary discourse or morally trusted; that, for mysterious if transcendental reasons, the whole "Nigra" kit-n-kaboodle, while a matter of decency, was absolutely unspeakable. Insofar as I am thoroughly formed by segregation, I got it mostly from these two exceptionally good and beloved people, who never mentioned it. Once I entered recovery from racism and other malignancies of spirit, I sprouted a cancer of rage against Kitty and Daddy. Though I was in my thirties, it was adolescent resentment for their having been with me, but fatefully before me, products of our times. As I was never able to confess this or work through it with them, it remains one of my chief regrets.

At church I learned the divine mandate ordaining separation of the races. My teachers pointed out aspects of biblical law and stories of Scripture which mandate separation. They didn't acknowledge that the separation in question was between Hebrews and indigenous Semitic peoples of the eastern Mediterranean, nor did that occur to me. They simply emphasized that the survival of the people of God depended on "keeping separate."

While no teacher advocated slavery, they seemed to emphasize regulations regarding slavery. I think I've always known who Philemon and Onesimus were: Philemon was Paul's friend, and Onesimus was Philemon's runaway slave, a Christian convert. Onesimus was sent back to Philemon with Paul's letter, later a book of Scripture, entreating the aggrieved master to accept his wayward chattel's promise, as a Christian, to be a good slave.

I grew up in the secure belief that my Dixie forebears, while tragically losing the "War Between the States," were not actually wrong about slavery. I learned at church that all biblical heroes were slave-holding males. "God's Son," and indeed God, are male. All biblical preachers of God are male. I learned there was something ominously "tempting" and disgusting about women in ways inscrutable to me, and that God therefore hedged women with more rules than men. Thus it was that the Bible and its Buckhead teachers drew me deeper into my Original Sin.

Living in Sin

I occasionally disobeyed my parents. Since I was their only child, adored and fawned over, they saw eye to eye with me on most things and didn't lay down much law. But I wasn't perfect. Kitty would cry when I "disappointed" her. Daddy would sigh.

For instance, I achieved sadistic pleasure from making Barbara Lynn, my little cousin, bawl. She did it with her mouth wide open. I put marbles in there, a perversity rooted in natal sinfulness. Furthermore, I usually manipulated the situation so that her bawling seemed to be her own or her sister's fault.

When I was in the seventh grade, I got the first shocking indication that I might be less than perfect. We were riding in our new red and white '52 Ford. Casually, my parents mentioned that they were getting me braces, "for your smile. And we're getting plastic surgery for your ears."

What's wrong with my "nicely bucked" teeth? What's wrong with my ears that I should have plastic ears? These were my thoughts, though, since we didn't talk about things, I didn't speak them. Actually, the space behind my bucked teeth was the width of my thumb, and my ears, which didn't crease at the joint with my head, stuck straight out like a dog's. Childhood pictures of me are goofy. My earliest parental training was that the teasing I was bound to receive regarding ears and teeth was actually a sign of public affection and should be well received (a bunch of crap I actually believed), and that in fact served me well during a lifetime of verbal abuse for quite different matters than ears and teeth. The orthodontic and plastic surgical rearrangement of my appearance was major, involving three years with a dentist who had hands the size of catchers' mitts and a year of bandages that made my head the size of a football helmet.

Worst of my earliest sins were the turtle races. My neighbor Bev and I collected box turtles her dad, a traveling salesman, found on the highway. We built pens in our yards. With a dozen or so between us, bored watching them poke out their heads and plod about, we invented the infamous turtle race. We drew a circle, pasted numbers on the colorful shells, set our dozen under an inverted basket, and after Bev's imitation of the Kentucky Derby bugle, lifted the basket and off they'd go. It took awhile for even the fastest to go very far, by which time we'd be hooting. Just before he or she (we never mastered the intimacies of box turtle gender) reached the curving line, some failure of killer instinct would intervene. The creature would turn back. Sometimes one would actually seem to follow the line. The tension was delicious.

It wasn't the races themselves. Word got out and we raised a crowd of roustabouts who got hooked, not on the lumbering sport but on the gambling. We required a nickel bet, raking a penny off the top. Unfortunately, disastrously really, Kitty caught us. The fact that gambling was one of the worst things to do had not yet been revealed to me. I'll have to admit it did give off the whiff of sulfur: the thrill of chance, greedy lust for victory, the cruel satisfaction from a neighbor's downfall, an aroma of ill-gotten gain from the mounting penny piles of profit, the orgy of mass disappointment. Kitty's solution was to bet bottle caps instead of nickels—an end to profits, and tragically, the races. The sensation was the specter of transgression. Thus I learned that Sin isn't just from being born in it. It comes after you. And we were in it together.

However naïve, my spirituality had a seriousness about it. As I said, I was born Born Again. I wanted to be a preacher. I read my Bible every night from the time I could read, and though I often fell asleep doing it and didn't understand much, there was something profound going on that went beyond the obscure words. Praying for Popo implanted in my soul the notion that war was sacred. Like the Bible, prayers for Popo and war entwined me with God. I began to notice how the best stories in my Bible were about God granting victory to soldiers like my uncle. Popo did survive the war, as I had prayed. But not all my prayers did so well.

When I was seven, Granddaddy, Kitty's daddy, had a stroke that shattered the right side of his brain. The stroke spared his witty Irish mind, but paralyzed and stiffened his entire left side, inflicting him with agonizing cramps which were mitigated only by generous shots of morphine. For the succeeding eleven years Nanny, a gracious, jolly butterball of loving warmth, rarely left his side, never for more than an hour, with but one three-day exception. She fed him by hand, turned him, bathed him and changed his sheets daily, tended his bodily functions with a native expertise that precluded even a single bedsore. She applied the daily syringe of morphine for half a decade, until a second stroke relieved the cramps.

Through massive doses of loving patience she then cured him of his addiction. She constantly chatted him up and sang to him. She watched the nation's first decade of television with him—her favorite was wrestling matches. She'd scream and weep at cruelties visited on such of her heroes as Gorgeous George. She paraded a host of guests (all of whom she stuffed with fried chicken, collards and the greasy like) through his tiny room, enjoyed with him their affection and profound admiration, and with them, his humor.

In all of this, Nanny was assisted every day either by Pearl Ridley, known to us as the quiet, regal "Tall Pearl," or by Pearl Nix, our "Fat Pearl," who was every bit as portly and jolly as Nanny. These two African American women are blazed on my memory. I did not "see" them or Nanny for two decades. They rather waited in the recesses of my conscience, a counterpoint to my demonic reduction of women to subservient incompetence, my caricature of black people as slovenly and slow-talking, to be awakened by masses of revolutionary blacks and women in another day.

My prayer-dance with God kept rhythm to the healing miracles of the Bible. In retrospect, I marvel at the spirituality of those days. I don't recall ever indulging in the confidence that Granddaddy would actually recover, though I urgently prayed that he would. Nor do I recall anger or loss of faith as years of illness wore on, even when he died in 1957. What I remember is a growing intensity and experienced closeness with God. There was an inchoate sense that God understood, even approved the passion of my unrelenting petitions. And though Granddaddy remained stiff, paralyzed and cramping, in the Great Mystery of my mind, I concluded that we were both receiving great blessing from my ineffectual prayers.

Saturdays were Cowboys and Indians movies at the Buckhead Theatre. From the time I could ride a bike, I was a regular, getting my earliest thrills from the slow slaughter of Western tribes by armed and lawless militias—my heroes. The big screen transmuted the armed terrorism and genocide into an exciting story of good versus evil, not at all unlike the gory war stories of the Bible my teachers regularly used to round up our chronically straying attention. My picture Bible was replete with color images of bloody violence, scenes that were taught at church and absorbed in nightly Bible readings. Decades later Kitty gave such a Bible to my children. She later asked them if they were enjoying it. Innocently, they told, to her horror, that their mother (not their peacenik father) had thrown it away.

In 1988 I was on a Korean bus headed for the Demilitarized Zone, tracing my route on a map. I recalled this map from grade school—the Korean War map! Grotesquely caricatured "North Korean Communists," faces of the enemy covered its northern half. Its south depicted heroic American soldiers—like Popo—no Koreans. The battle line was a red ribbon. Each day one of us (best days, me) studied the war in the paper and marked the day's advance or retreat with the ribbon. Advance brought football game cheers. At one point, the ribbon was nearly to "Red China," heady days of near-delirium.

For a while, retreats were regular and ominous. I recall the feeling of sick dread when we heard of an impending "Communist takeover," as if Koreans were approaching Buckhead to confiscate our Bibles and bomb our churches. Our public school teacher would pray for the defeat of the Communists "in Jesus' precious name."

Daddy and Lay's Potato Chips

I accompanied Daddy to work on Saturdays. He recorded the week's income on a manual adding machine. For three hours he clicked away at the keys and pulled the hand-crank, a rolling tape of added figures scrolling out. Daddy's office opened onto the alcove of Betty Childs, the secretary he shared with Herman, and to the accounting department which consisted of ten desks crowded closely together. The accountants called Daddy "Mr. George." Herman was "Mr. Lay."

This was in the old Lay's headquarters, corner of Houston and Boulevard, overlooking tall downtown buildings (one was twenty stories, the "tallest in the south") half a mile away. Lay's was a two-story brick building, and the offices were on the second floor front. The back and the first floor were the plant where many of the potato and corn chips eaten in the central Southeast were fried. Potatoes were poured into two long conveyor-belted vats at one end, steaming crisp chips drawn up the other. These were spilled into waiting bags which were automatically sealed, dropped into cardboard boxes and rolled out to trucks at the dock. It was quiet Saturdays—too bad for me. Nothing was more exciting than its roaring operation, and nothing tastier than hot chips off the belt. Saturdays were imagination time, of chips pouring into bags, trucks pulling out to fan across the region and returning money for Daddy and me to compile. I typed numbers he'd copied by hand into his annual ledger book, pulled the handle to crunch them and print totals. I sat at Betty's window, gazed at the tall buildings, or roamed the plant, stole chips from an unfilled box, thought about people who worked there and called Daddy "Mr. George." Nothing I did in a busy boyhood week was as thrilling as going to work with Daddy on Saturdays.

Between the plant and downtown is the neighborhood Black folk call "Sweet Auburn." Daddy didn't know that name. He referred to it as "the Nigra section" or "Shanty Town," giving the unmistakable message it was dangerous, somehow defiled. Even when I purposely looked I didn't see "the Nigra section" or "Shanty Town" in Sweet Auburn. This was early in the decade before Brown v. Board of Education, racist culture in full sway, utterly, quietly segregated. Sweet Auburn was dominated by two "Nigra" churches, whose names struck my whiteboy ears as characteristically "Nigra" in other words, comical.

I recall my confusion that these people we were to keep separate from (the Bible called them "Heathen") actually had churches. The larger was Big Bethel; the other Ebenezer. White Atlanta and I didn't know that the pastor of Ebenezer was Rev. Martin Luther King, Sr., or "Daddy King" as he'd become a decade later, when his oldest son of the same name became world famous. I first heard of Daddy King in 1969, after I had become a devoted follower of his son. It was a couple days after I drove to Memphis, to the Lorraine Motel, the morning after his son was shot dead. I'd gone to march with the garbage workers in the mournfullest procession that ever there was. I learned of Daddy King when I watched his son's funeral, broadcast worldwide from Ebenezer in Sweet Auburn, two blocks from the Lay's Potato Chips plant.

I had never been to Sweet Auburn. It was not in my world. I knew it only as "Shanty Town," Daddy's image of black housing. Years later I discovered Sweet Auburn to be an upper-middle-class neighborhood beneath the rising towers of booming Atlanta. I first visited there much later, two decades into peace and justice activism. After meetings at the Martin Luther King Center for Nonviolent Social Change, I battled crowds of tourists at the King home, larger and nicer than our first two Buckhead houses. Even then I did not place the house or Sweet Auburn on my personal landscape. That revelation dawned twenty years later after I preached at the new Ebenezer Cathedral. I drove out the church parking lot, under the large brass sign marking entrance to the Martin Luther King National Historic Site. And there, directly across the street, was my childhood second home: the old Lay's plant.

SOUTHERN BAPTIST SEX

Being Born in Sin never bothered me until a few years after I'd been baptized, when several nasties struck in quick succession. One was a bizarre adventure with Daddy near my twelfth birthday. Sunday after worship he stopped by the church library and checked out two books—something I'd never seen him do.

Daddy grimly handed me one of them—he'd not given me a book before— said we'd talk "next Sunday." It was about the birds and the bees—literally. I struggled through it. It was deadly boring, and so far as I could tell, pointless. Next Sunday he asked if I'd read it and gave me the second book, even more grimly. This one was horrifying, describing the ordeal that married people have to endure if they want children. It had to do with nakedness, urination and terminal embarrassment, enough to frighten anyone off from the idea of marriage, let alone children.

When he asked a week later if I had any questions, I couldn't muster a single word. That was it. I concluded that a dreadful fate awaited me—something that deeply disturbed my supremely imperturbable father. What I also took away, though neither the books nor Daddy actually said so, was that sex, according to the Bible, was somehow evil.

Although within the norm of maturation tales, I thought the following troubling occurrences off the charts at the time. I had an impassioned dream of Sally, a classmate I hadn't particularly noticed as a girl. The dream salaciously revealed her gender, and as for the first time, her creamy skin, newly sprouted curves and swanlike neck. I awoke deliciously strangling Sally. Where in God's name did that come from? It wasn't in Daddy's books.

Next, at the pool, I dunked Betsy, a dark pixie of a preteen on whom I had a painful crush. There she was, suddenly, unaccountably present. The word "flesh" comes to mind, recently ripened, tauntingly, impossibly in reach like Sally's in the dream. Betsy ignored me, so I pulled her by her black hair under the water and held her under. Buster Toby, a kid in my grade, somehow wrenched me away and gave me a tongue-lashing. Betsy was coughing, crying, and I was stunned speechless with horror at what I had done. However much her "flesh" and imperious disregard might insult me, however dreadful this insurrection in my wayward body, I was showing off that I was bigger, stronger. I could grasp her seductive swimming-pool self and gratify myself with the twin thrill of touch and vengeance—two full decades before I learned the word "misogyny."

KITTY AND MISOGYNY

Preachers since Apostle Paul attribute Original Sin to Eve and subsequent mothers. So it was with me. I was born knowing this from the Bible. But I was also born, without knowing it for decades, in a wicked morass which set me crosswise to gender through Kitty.

I never called her "Mother. " Daddy called her "Sugar Lump." We adored and sacralized Kitty—five feet, one hundred pounds of integrity, competence, generosity and grace. But my adoration was also a medium for condescension, disrespect, even emotional domination.

Like priests elevating the Host, we lifted her up, it seeming neither her place nor power to hold herself up. She belonged to us. She gave me literally everything I wanted. She was tiny. Conceding to physical reality, she eschewed corporal punishment. Her last spanking in response to my sassy retort was so painless that we both collapsed in laughter. Her teary emotionality, in contrast to Daddy's steely stoicism, was cast by them as emotional weakness. She admired Daddy and deferred to him in "serious things."

We assumed that practicality and intelligence belonged to men, not to consecrated women. I don't recall as a child seeing her read a book or newspaper. Both parents were anti-intellectual. But I respected and emulated Daddy's philistine populism as a principled choice. Kitty's version, for instance, her derisive superior laughter at things she didn't grasp, influenced by Daddy's sighs of condescension, I judged, simply, as simple. Her charisma with children, rock-star popularity with my friends, easy domestic competence, her genuineness and tendency to light up a crowd, lifted me toward respect and pride and formed a major element of who I would become. But there was a spiritual quicksand sucking me down. It folded over the whole of her with a benignly comical persona. "I'm just a kid at heart," she'd say with her great laugh. And I'd laugh, as if my mother were congenitally immature.

Writing this is wrenching and shameful. Given our closeness and affection, she'd be baffled by it and deeply hurt. My recovery, unraveling the evil complex of my formation, turned me against her. She died before I'd done enough to make confession.

It wasn't her fault. We lived this way in a context which offered no alternatives. The only women professionals in Buckhead were "schoolteachers," often characterized "old maids," in other words, unable to attract husbands. Teaching was "women's work." Even male teachers, always identified as such, did "women's work." Nurses and secretaries, all female, were considered mere helpers in congenital subservience to respected males. No woman held a leadership position in any church I knew of, and none were or aspired to be religious professionals. The greatest woman of our time, Eleanor Roosevelt, was a caricature in our house: warbly voice, awkward public manner, the opposite of sexual and attractive, transmuted from the best to the worst of womanhood. She was a wife and reputedly a mother, but who she was wife to, the "socialist" with seemingly permanent claim on the White House, Daddy despised. Eleanor Roosevelt never emerged for me through the malign fog.

Women probably regard my confessions as more or less inconsequential, somewhere between insulting and laughable. I'm a minor cog in a great wheel that has fatefully disadvantaged women throughout recorded history, fully exposed by contemporary women, wrenching me around. My recollections represent what it was like to be this individual instance of what, more or less, we all were.

Anti-Semitism and Bigotry

I grew up believing the Baptist doctrine that Jews were God's Chosen People. Yet the New Testament says they rejected, then crucified, Jesus, thereby falling from Grace. I didn't encounter any actual Jews until high school. I credited what I'd heard at church, that they were "lost," but since Catholics were also lost, as were kids who didn't go to church, the four Jews in my class of two hundred hardly made a ripple in that massive category.

I accidentally fell into friendship with Ike Blumberg, one of the four. A third of the squirmy sperm which went into the formation of my nascent anti-Semitic serpent—the other two being Bible and Sunday School—had to do with him. Kitty, hearing his name, assumed a dramatically, uncharacteristically portentous persona to say I "shouldn't go to Ike's." Why? She hadn't the vocabulary to say "Defiled," but I got from implications of her inarticulation that it would be blasphemous, somehow dangerous. I didn't go back.

Because of the Bible and what I learned in Sunday School, anti-Semitism seemed somehow religious. God's Chosen People were at the center of a colossal Mystery. Jesus, who in The Mystery was more or less God, was inescapably Jewish, as were his twelve disciples. God, The Ground of Being, somehow was, too. Yet the Jewish people, in God's eternal Plan of Redemption, bore responsibility for the sacrificial slaughter of Jesus for my Salvation, and universal enmity for the Church. This Mystery was borne into my time on the slender shoulders of little Ike Blumberg and the aura of defilement upon his house.

Another friend was Jim Phillips. Our only "Jim," he was a setup when we read of "Nigger Jim," Huck Finn's epic traveling companion. Our "Jim" was thus renamed by catcalling howls from a pack of adolescent Southern whiteboys. Thus it was that an anti-slavery classic contributed its thread to the fabric of Sin into which I was born. I remember tentative embarrassment the first time I used the name. Even I knew better.

I own this word in shame as a significant part of my history. I presume to use it here, though I recognize that it is offensive to my African American friends. It's a confession, letting the brutality of the guttural, its disrespectful corruption of "Negro," hang out from the base of who I am. On more than one occasion, I hailed Jim with the epithet in the school hallway (to be answered by an African American janitor who for meager wages kept our prodigious trash from underfoot) then laughed about it with partners in infamy.

"Let Justice roll down ..."

When I was a High School "sub-freshman" (eighth-grader), I trashed the grammar school. Jim and I and two others were roaming one dark night and found ourselves at the school where we noticed an open second floor window. I was gifted at climbing. It was as if my little vertical talent turned against me. I bragged that the window was within range, and with their skeptical encouragement, I hoisted myself up and in. I ran down the stairs and flung wide the door to admit them. We upended desks, emptied teachers' drawers, pushed infirmary mattresses down stairs and unrolled for the length of the long hall reels of sixteen millimeter films from the projection room. The only explanation I ever came up with for wreaking havoc that dark night is Born in Sin. What I felt wasn't guilt. That came later. It was the sweet, erotic buzz of pride.

Thus I discovered the biblical Prophets. I had memorized a fair number of their sayings. Most were about Christmas: "A virgin shall conceive ...," "Unto us a child is born ...," etc. Repeating them, especially around Nanny's Christmas tree, awakened my little mind to the wonder of this grand drama, allegedly "prophesied" centuries before by these alleged seers. I would later stumble into the academic study of the Bible, and learn that the Prophets weren't talking about Christmas at all, and hadn't foretold Jesus.

One of the prophetic sayings I learned was "Let Justice roll down like waters, and righteousness as an ever-flowing stream," which clearly had nothing to do with Christmas, and came distressingly to mind in the wake of our break-in.

Ten years older than me, Martin Luther King was a kid studying Bible verses at Ebenezer when I was a block from him at the Lay's plant. He too memorized this "Let Justice roll down ..." passage, but his later prophetic insights about a host of evils more fateful than school trashings shamed me far more. After hearing him speak decades later, I became obsessed with the Prophets.

Their words shaped and sharpened my concerns more than any source.

Dr. King's worldwide image was interpreted and dominated by media people and historians who were typically not Christian, nor sophisticated in either liberal or Black Church Christianity. In black and liberal mainstream churches Dr. King is considered a reincarnation of the Hebrew Prophets. Even some Jewish theologians think of him that way, as does Taylor Branch in his Pulitzer Prize-winning secular history *The King Years.* I certainly do. All the biblical Prophets were ordinary people with flaws, who, like Dr. King, were propelled by the unique circumstances of their historical moment.

I was morally, spiritually, emotionally and theologically upended by the series of social movements to be described in this book. The first and most fateful of these was the Civil Rights Movement—an uprising of black people, especially black church people. In my considered opinion, the result of a lifetime both of intense relevant experience and disciplined study (shared by Taylor Branch and most others) King's leadership was the single most important of the socioeconomic, political and religious factors which converged and resulted in the Civil Rights Movement. It's not that he was anything other than human. It's simply that he was the spark that lit the fire, and I was consumed by the fire. When he and I were both children down the street, I could not have imagined anyone like him. The cultural distance of the hundred yards or so between us mirrored the central peculiarity of American history.

Back then, alongside the pride for what I got away with in the elementary school, was a very real dread that somehow "Justice" was about to "roll down" on me "like waters." It did not—or has not yet. My only consequence has been the above-mentioned guilt, actually far worse now than then. Also, I received a memorable tongue-lashing from my wife when she first learned about it by reading a draft of this book.

MY TOTEM: NOT DANCING FOR GOD

Upon the delayed dawning of puberty, such as it was, Kitty sent me to Freddie Foote's Dancing School. Cool kids went to Margaret's in Buckhead. Buckhead was then suburban Atlanta, Foote's nearly to town. You had to ride the bus. A consequence of being born Born Again is you're not very cool. Nobody was at Foote's. I have no idea how Kitty found the place—maybe at church.

High school dances were her platform of glory. Given her bounce, fluidity and utter unreserve in the dancing regularly triggered by music on the kitchen radio, I believed it. What I couldn't imagine was Daddy as her partner. He was pretty much her opposite choreographically. I was like him. I never saw him dance with her, a deprivation she took out on me. She grabbed me up when jitterbug flew from our kitchen airways. I suffered these as attacks, and given a repressed eroticism under our bond, the Freudian in my immaturity, it was clumsily grotesque. Hence Freddie Foote's.

I couldn't not watch the cool Margaret's-bound kids and their hormones from my arid wilderness. I remember mounting and dismounting the bus, slumping up the walkway to a dreary converted residence, dragging a book bag as if being marched to my doom. All of us were mostly asexual. Girls had pimply faces, clammy right hands which I had to hold with a clammy left, bony spines where I slapped the other one. Their feet plodded directly on mine as we went, "step together, step together, back-and," round the dismal room. I'd rather be in hell.

That summer our youth group went to Ridgecrest Baptist Assembly. Talk about hormones! They ricocheted off awesome mountains, soiling for my recoiling immaturity the old-time erotic religiosity for which I came. I mostly stayed apart.

On a sultry afternoon I stumbled on some gingham-clad mountaineer kids who didn't, as a matter of religious commitment, dance. Not ever. This struck me as a staggering Christian witness exceeding my own; even Hilda's, who went to Margaret's and, in the jitterbug, reminded me strongly of Kitty. That night at the huge, open-air evangelistic service, God's Creation towering above, its fragrance sweetening my heavy breathing, I "went forward" to Give up Dancing for God.

I read Freud a decade later at Yale Divinity School—one of several "Aha! Moments" to punctuate my jerky pilgrimage. There was psycho-sexual development, oedipal conflict, repression, and transference, the secular theology of psychoanalysis, how a growing boy could subconsciously fall in love with his mother, be scandalized by such a thing in the crawlies beneath his thoughts, pursue a desperate life-search for escape which wouldn't destroy his mother or eviscerate his father, and how by giving up dancing for God, I resolved it all. What could she say? Her preacher boy had become a saint. As an oedipal solution, however, it had disastrous side effects, removing from my path a natural bridge toward sexual maturity.

I was the only kid in Buckhead who didn't dance—for God or any other reason. Though peers gave me aloof, bemused respect, it set me apart. I became more nerdy and lonely. I was left grievous, wandering for dark hours alone during school dances, trying not to have what I called dirty thoughts. At two more or less obligatory dances, I subjected first one then another beautiful, popular girl, who surely thought that my invitation meant I'd abandoned my curious vow, to the humiliation of sitting out the dances with me for an agonizing evening.

But it really was for God, not just Freud. I read Joseph Campbell and Mercea Eliade. "Aha!" again. People inhabit symbols and rituals to touch transcendence. I read Paul Tillich: God as understood by Christians is known only in imperfect, simpleminded, symbols. And Karl Jung: Symbols have reality in a depth of consciousness shared with everyone, but to access them often manifests more or less bizarre behavior—such as not-dancing-for-God. Bizarre sure enough.

Whatever it solved in relation to Kitty, delayed adolescent

sexuality and social clumsiness, it put me in profound touch with that which in transcendence I knew as God. Campbell and Eliade gave a word from earlier cultures:"Totem." Not-dancing-for-God was my totem. I thought of myself in terms of Samson. Not his huge muscles, but his long hair, his totem, a quirky public symbol. It signified to the world, but more significantly to himself that he was God's man. There was enormous strength, being God's man. I "didn't dance"... for God. I was God's kid. In the bizarreness, I got strength.

Face of the Jim Crow Enemy

I didn't dance, for God, the face of my totem. But its reality was a larger metabolism of biblical mandates by which I intended to live. While not-dancing I also tried "manfully" to "not look on a woman to lust." I prayed for our soldiers fighting for God's people. And I kept "separate."

When I was a high school freshman, Chief Justice Earl Warren entered my life, and when a sophomore, Rosa Parks and Martin Luther King. May 17, 1954, *Brown v. Board of Education* was read by Justice Warren. The next day it rained. I remember standing at a window at North Fulton High School. Glowering clouds streaked the glass with heavy raindrops, like tears streaming down, mud puddles splashing beyond it. I'd never met a black kid—had only seen a few in "Shanty Town" out Daddy's window. Standing at that tear-stained window, I imagined a flood of African Americans, overwhelming North Fulton like dark raindrops. From then until long after I was catapulted to the other side of the issue, the only billboard more ubiquitous on my landscape than "Burma Shave" and "See Rock City Atop Lookout Mountain" was "Impeach Earl Warren."

My sophomore year no black kid entered North Fulton or any Southern school, so I became more concerned with my own life. But then Rosa Parks splashed across *Atlanta Journal* headlines, and I began to worry again. Four days later blacks boycotted Montgomery buses and a subversive "Montgomery Improvement Association" was formed. The new pastor of a Montgomery Baptist Church, just down from seminary up north, a name I didn't recognize, was elected its leader. Ironically, he was the kid who'd grown up in the Ebenezer Church parsonage out Daddy's window.

Fading memory suggests Ralph Bunche was the first prominent black to invade my crimped awareness. I'd heard of Booker T. Washington, George Washington Carver, "Nigra colleges" downtown, but only as ironic anomalies. I heard a mix of resentment and pride that Atlanta had "more Nigra millionaires than any city in the nation," resentment that any had achieved what we hadn't and pride that they were bought off by our noblesse oblige. I didn't know Lena Horne was a movie star, recording artist, and the most beautiful of women. She was edited out of our films, not played on Dixie radio, her records unavailable.

I didn't know about Marian Anderson, Fats Waller, Duke Ellington, nor of Louis Armstrong's significance. I never heard of Langston Hughes, Fannie Lou Hamer or Tuskegee Airmen. Sports pages mentioned that Jackie Robinson had integrated baseball, but said nothing about his moral heroism. Nor of W.E.B. Dubois, Marcus Garvey, Harriet Tubman or Sojourner Truth. I knew about Rev. Adam Clayton Powell who was depicted as a big-time "Nigra preacher," chauffeured in an entourage of Cadillacs with prominence in "the corrupt Nigra church," elected to "disgrace" the halls of Congress by "Yankee politics." There was a lot in the papers about Thurgood Marshall, a black lawyer who'd successfully persuaded a unanimous, all-white US Supreme Court to issue the most unthinkable of decisions. With these precedents my cluttered mind received its initial image of Martin Luther King, mediated by Dixie media and the common sense of bigoted gossip.

I've mentioned *Faces of the Enemy*. I was old enough during wartime to have been determined by those images. But what struck me when I read the book was more grotesque distortions of Dr. King that appeared during and after the Montgomery Bus Boycott, and that I "saw" regularly on the round, twelve-inch screen of our Zenith TV, in newsreels preceding movies and in photos in the *Atlanta Constitution*.

An exception underscores the perversity of my formation. Daddy taught me to appreciate Ralph McGill—the beginning of my fascination with the written word. McGill, a Pulitzer-winning southern moderate, was editor of the *Atlanta Constitution*. Daddy wasn't a reader, but the flow of McGill's prose drew him in, and he showed me. Every morning, I'd bring in the paper. He and I would drink in the latest McGill. Never did McGill advocate King or the

Movement, but neither did he vilify them. Still, much as I loved to read him, his neutral imagery did nothing to soften the "face" of this "enemy" in my mind. I "saw" a raging flamboyant spectacle, in a street (never a church) surrounded by a throbbing mob of either angry or arrogantly jubilant black faces: curling upper lip, flashing carnivorous teeth, threateningly up-thrust fists. I heard screaming, a rhythmical cadence evocative of African predators and jungle drums, clips of oratorical phrases outrageous to the point of treason. Buckhead discourse was peppered with exclamations that this demagogue was The Anti-Christ.

The media did not mention King's PhD. We never heard his biblical preaching, the prayers or Baptist hymns he led or the passion of the singing, never heard an unedited sentence, let alone a paragraph from his charismatic oratory, never his prophetic reasoning, explication of its foundation in Scripture, nor his compassion for people like me. None of that. Just skillfully selected caricatures of a raging crazy man— clearly the face of the enemy.

I had no concept of him as the seminal theologian of twentieth-century Christianity, reincarnation of biblical prophets, herald of justice, architect with Gandhi of Nonviolent Social Change, Nobel laureate, icon of a national holiday, hero now to two generations across the planet. Even as a convert and follower at great distance I never really "saw" Dr. King, though I did meet him when he received the Dahlberg Peace Prize at the American Baptist Churches Biennial Convention of 1964, among the first of countless recognitions. It took decades for this moral giant to penetrate the marrow of my consciousness.

In time I read his books, one at a time for a while, then all together. I read a Pulitzer Prize-winning book about him, and Jim Cone's theological treatise on King and Malcolm X, peeling away distorting preconceptions. I had the incalculable privilege of late night, bourbon-lubricated conversations with an aging Ralph Abernathy and other Movement heroes who revealed the man himself. But I was Born in Sin with a heritage of attitudes bequeathed to the cultural limitations of our journalists and their readership: economic tentacles of Dixie businesses which bought ads and set limits on coverage, the function of Jim Crow media to contain "the Nigra Problem," the social psychology of daily conversation taking place in the wake of slave-holding, residual bitterness about the Civil War defeat, still-redolent Reconstruction humiliation and multiform accommodations of twentieth century racism. And, Kitty and Daddy.

CLIFF AND THE SPORT OF SACRILEGE

Something else was going on in my life which would have more to do with my totem than Not-Dancing. It was friendship with Cliff Hendrix, a lanky, homely, Dixie-drawling humorist with grease under his fingernails. One thing was his hobby, where he got the grease. Mine was electric trains. His, more absorbing and impressive, was restoring a '27 Marmon, a jalopy he'd rescued from the junkyard.

In the din of shrieking tree frogs, we tromped the woods after church on Sunday nights. One time Cliff cocked a grin and said, "If Samson was like Dr. Swilley said, he was a juvenile delinquent!" He slapped his leg, exploding in his great roar, then went on a mental treasure hunt in Samson's bio to expose him as badder than us. Thus began a Sunday night escapade. We'd forsake holy precincts for a favorite grove (and no Christians) to de-sacralize Scripture and laugh our heads off. In gossipy lust for pungent detail, to the buzz-saw of crickets and katydids, we rescued vile and funny characters from Dr. Swilley's pious spin on inflated Bible language.

We howled, gasping scents of honeysuckle, at every stray hint that these were real people who farted and belched. Elijah "went aside" in other words, took a crap. Jacob cheated his brother. Old Abraham huffed and puffed sex. Moses set a bush on fire. Adam and Eve snatched at fig leaves to cover up. The best story, the one that left Cliff holding his stomach and rolling on the ground, was David on his deathbed. Doctors put a naked woman under the covers to see if he was dead yet. He was. Sins on New Testament pages were less fun, except Jesus at the Cana wedding bootlegging and guzzling nine hundred gallons of wine—count them.

I was one hell of a holy kid, but these devious exploits into the biblical underworld did a number on my piety. As I grew into girl smells, sidelong glances and embarrassing truths, I unearthed buried evidence that these characters writhed in guilts like mine. I began to finger a blurring line between religion and corruption, the broad river on which the flotsam and jetsam of life are flowing, wherever they tend.

The grove of our Bible-trashing was the kudzu tangle where I'd formerly snuck off to walk and talk with Jesus. Like the Smoky Mountains north of Buckhead, this little wooded spot was akin to the Sanctuary at Second-Ponce de Leon church, my sacred space. What I'd later embrace as natural wonderlands were back then simply where Jesus was, transformed into an improvisational theater for laughing at the Bible. I failed to notice, but not long after I first laughed at the Bible with Cliff, I stopped walking and talking with Jesus.

Cliff and I worked construction for a dollar an hour. We were too dumb to know that building, supplying and tearing down five-story scaffolds was insanely unsafe. As for dumb, a mason once shouted, "Williamson, get me a brick-bender to go around this corner."

"What's a brick-bender, Sir?"

"You goddamnedsonofabitchignoramusasshole. Get your butt down and ask the boss." I went down, but knew better than to ask the boss. After half an hour tossing the tool shed for the brick-bender, who should pop his head in but the boss.

"What the hell?"

"Looking for the brick-bender. Sir."

"You goddamnedsonofabitchignoramusasshole, get your butt up that scaffold and don't come down."

Given that I fall a lot, it's a wonder I never fell off or brought the whole scaffold down, perched as it was on a downhill slope atop a pile of blocks. Besides the priceless experience, and the hourly dollar, the main thing we got was an expanded vocabulary and insight into the raucous, earthy humanity of builders in the Bible—like Jesus.

LAUGHING AT THE BIBLE

It was the Buckhead Sunday nights with Cliff and the lightning bugs, laughing at the Bible, lifting the grey veil of piety shadowing its pages, skirting their supernatural outcomes, engaging them with self, that I first got upended in Grace.

We were reckless, risked taboos, put our ruddy selves into the thick of it. It was just a bit of forbidden fun. I actually had no idea there was significance in this impious clowning. But there was. Discovering it would take several decades. Borrowing from those decades still to come, I can say we were engaging Scripture with imagination in order "to know" it.

"To know" in Hebrew means not just get facts, but make love, take in with cathartic feeling, sleep with. It includes even hate, as in Job and Jeremiah. It's rational as far as reason goes. Truth comes up. But it's not based in or counting on reason. It's frankly subjective, psychological, but not in the end. To know is finally to know YHWH, who cannot be known, whose ways are not our ways, nor thoughts our thoughts. "To know" starts and ends with faith. Nothing can be known that isn't a risk to know, isn't surrendered to, lived out. Westerners don't "know" that way. We imagine that way. Imagination is closest in our repertoire to Hebrew "knowledge." We imagine God who cannot be known. But we never think to compare imagination to knowledge because Hebrew Scripture treats knowledge with such awe. We don't regard imagination so highly. It's something we do on the sly—play. What we admire is work.

"To know" the Bible with Cliff, a book of colorful characters and suggestive images, was to interpret with imagination. Like me and Cliff, Hebrew nomads circled up around blazing campfires. To the fracas of children running in and out, they played with sacred stories, their sole entertainment, for fun, telling it differently in different tellers' imaginations. Christians told Jesus stories in church. Gospel authors wrote stories heard there as each imagined them. How differently imagined, for instance, are Luke and John. Paul was deadly serious with the Hebrew Bible until, traumatically converted as I repeatedly was, he turned his imagination loose. His imagination with Bible stories is as fateful as was his mind with Jesus stories. Methods of interpretation, of the Bible as of life, are reductions for alien purposes anyway. So why not have a little fun, take risks? Like me and Cliff. Amazing Grace.

My adventures with Cliff had no immediate effect on my radically biblical-kid persona. Just before college, I was selected Youth Pastor at church, as Hilda was just a girl and wasn't eligible. Second-Ponce de Leon was a 4,000 member church with a huge budget. The primary goal of Southern Baptists was growth in the number and financial contributions of members. They were prolific with gimmicks for both. "Pack the Pew Plan" was the current one, meaning to fill up the pew with new people. My being Youth Pastor meant I would give the Sunday morning sermon, normally attended by about 1,600 people, packing the pews.

Ironic Cliff expressed regret that with a preacher like me instead of the popular Dr. Swilley, the pews would be empty, and disappoint the church plan. He was, of course, right. Cliff decried the pending disaster to our "PPP Spiritual Statistics," the scant drawing power of "a roustabout from North Fulton High." I suggested we substitute "A Pew for You Plan."

"Never happen" Cliff decreed. "A Pew or Two for You," he howled, and slapped his knee.

Indeed. It was a humiliatingly empty sanctuary, first of several thousand ecclesiastical failures. In my inaugural sermon, "Gimme that Old-Time Religion," I out-fundamentalized the church, already the angry young man.

Giving up Not Dancing for God, for God

When I went to college, I chose Wake Forest (Baptist) College where buildings looked like church and dancing wasn't allowed. I was tired of being bizarre, of living where doing anything overtly for God was a curiosity. I went where I could live in a landscape of churches and not-dance with the best of them.

What I got was more or less the polar opposite. My first discovery was that everyone danced. I was still the only one abstaining. And those buildings weren't churches or remotely like churches. Most fellow Demon Deacons didn't even go to church. Moreover, a movement to overturn the no-dancing-on-campus rule had the college in delirium.

I hadn't come out with the scandal of my totem, so I was able to squat on the sidelines of political debates incognito. What I heard amounted to the first, and among the most memorable insights of an inexcusably long academic career. It was delivered by my roommate, Charlie Chatham from Buckhead. Charlie, by ironic coincidence, went to Margaret's and was her most accomplished dancer.

More ironic still, he was Kitty's favorite. More frequently and wholeheartedly than me, he was her kitchen jitterbug partner. The particular initial insight he delivered through the chattering politics was an eloquent "It isn't fair!"

Precisely what was not fair, according to Charlie, was for Baptists to impose their "moralistic bigotry" on students with perfectly fine beliefs, which would never include not-dancing. Of course, he was right. It wasn't fair. And I certainly didn't want "moralistic" and "bigotry" applied to me. Being fair was among the chief Christian virtues both parents had advocated. They'd draped me with laurels for being fair, my having got away with the marbles unfairly administered to Barbara Lynn. My not-dancing never hurt anybody, except of course, my beautiful dates for those dances. I was anything but moralistic as I persuaded one un-danced-with-girl (after not-dancing all evening) to go to Stone Mountain for a night-long, sexually immature make-out session.

My commitment to not-dancing had nothing to do with bigotry, moralism or sex. It was a sign, a totem, a shock of Samsonian long hair, marking me God's kid. The last thing God's kid should be is not fair! So I joined the movement to overturn the no-dancing rule.

It began here! Being upended by and then joining social movements would become the story of my life, hence of this memoir. On about the most famous day in Wake Forest history, we marched out of obligatory chapel and on the administration building terrace, staged a dance. There before cameras of *NBC* and *Life Magazine* I Gave Up Not-Dancing-for-God, for God!— the most inspired and empowering thing I'd yet done.

When the euphoria wore off, however, I discovered that I had lost my totem. Not-not-dancing-for-God, for-God, didn't cut it. Like Samson when Delilah cut his hair, I lost my strength. I'd get it back, but not soon. It would be a third of a century before I'd grasp the significance of the Dancing-on-Campus-Movement-Day.

My Soul Versus Moby Dick

A week into Wake, Mac Bryan, a craggy prophet and religion professor who would achieve a central role in my maturation, asked if the earth was created in seven days. I said it was. "Really?" he exclaimed, incredulous, and cackled. "Why on earth would you believe that?" he hooted. After a couple more classes and fits of cackling at my piety, I grew ashamed of "Gimme that Old-Time Religion." Something was happening to my soul.

Laughing at the Bible with Cliff was my total literary involvement. English, not to mention Latin at North Fulton, had awakened dread for the printed word. I was horrified at the first college English assignment: *Moby Dick*, a hundred pages! Not surviving fifty, I slunk to class, terminally unprepared, but something else happened.

It was the lecture, delivered by John Broderick, a slouching, drawling, unprepossessing young prof. Before he was finished, scales were pried from unseeing eyes, unaccountable thrill gurgling up my gut. This lazy-talking man, with words, awoke awe in my wilting soul for secular literature: *Moby Dick* no less! Rushing to my dorm's smelly confines I reread the assigned pages, and before the crack of dawn all umpteen hundred other pages, and with my raw soul witnessed an epic confrontation between human aspiration and cruel, unyielding, godless nature. I promptly changed my major from Religion to English.

Everybody's favorite class was Romantic Poets, taught by everybody's favorite dean, a soft-spoken, oval-faced Harvard *Wunderkind,* Ed Wilson, who was to become a campus icon and later the name on a campus building. I was still trembling with the exposé of academic Religion and thrill of secular literature, staggering from the loss of my totem, when he quoted Wordsworth's "Intimations of Immortality"—and gave name to my ordeal.

There was a time when meadow, grove, and stream,
The earth, and every common sight,
To me did seem
apparell'd in celestial light ...,
It is not now as it hath been of yore;
Turn wheresoe'er I may,
by night or day,
The things which I have seen I now can see no more...
But yet I know, where'er I go,
that there hath passed away a glory from the earth.

"Disenchantment" was the name. I began slow descent into a near-terminal case of it. I became a frat boy, quit church, embraced a young literateur and notoriously irreverent cynic named Clough. Me and Clough devoured Faulkner, Hemingway, Joyce, Salinger, Whitman, Dickinson, Eliot, experimenting with the intellectual. I dabbled in Existentialism and adopted radical politics. I wrote for the college newspaper, publishing a bitter satire on Billy Graham's sermon delivered in our required chapel service, depicting him as a vendor of pablum. I satirized the chaplain for his pompous prayers inveighed at football games. To an angry uproar I editorialized for the integration of the college. Ironically, "Nigger Jim," editor of his East Alabama University paper did as well.

These exploits were in keeping with the spirit of our fraternity, which lived in the glory of one of our brothers, graduated the year before I entered, who rigged an oversized bra to drop through a ceiling aperture in the chapel and dangle over the Baptist Convention president during his sermon. This was John Wagster, a six-foot-six-inch redhead I didn't meet until after I began dating his sister, Carol, whom I later married, John officiating.

During senior year, I did something that in retrospect is profoundly symbolic of who I'd be throughout my life. I, who a decade later would become chaplain of a college chapel, did a "protest lockup" of the Wake Forest Chapel. After a week of exhaustive, and if I may say, sophisticated preparation, three frat brothers and I executed our plan to lock a presumably grateful student body from chapel. We timed the rounds of night watchmen and estimated we could complete the lockup in an hour, between 2:00 and 3:00 in the morning. We procured lengths of chain and padlocks for doors.

After locking it all up from the inside, we exited through the choir loft door (which opened into a narrow space) by toppling a board in the well, jamming it. We then hid in nighttime bushes to watch the watchman make his unhappy discovery. He soon did, radioed for help (which quickly came, lights blazing), retrieved a heavy blunderbuss and before our watering eyes broke the door flat down. By dawn, chains were cut and doors opened wide for unsuspecting students. Thus my life: a quixotic endeavor to shoot down the intrusive presence of ubiquitous religion.

The story has a fittingly wacky conclusion. A week later I was summoned to the office of the Dean, Ed Wilson of Romantic Poets, by then my valiant defender both from predatory administrators and from myself. He told me that the watchman had noticed our frat house lights on at the time of the lockup. A brother was identified from a composite picture of our brotherhood, shown at hardware stores that sold and cut chains: Joe Hensley, a goofy-looking scarecrow of an adolescent, who was the Demon Deacon, our clownish college mascot. The Dean told me, the frat president, to tell the others a perpetrator was busted. The rest should turn themselves in. I thereupon turned myself in and dragged in the others. We had to buy the damn door—which, I proudly tell current Wake students, I like to think I own.

Then, born Born Again, I was Born Again again. I got arrested and went to jail.

It Isn't Fair

By Junior year, *Brown v. Board of Education* and the Bus Boycott were a half decade in the past, events I gave a token of emotional distress but not much thought. Thought began February 1, 1960. Having been without my totemic power for two years, I was sprawled on my frat house sofa watching the news. What I saw broadcast to the world was from Greensboro, thirty miles east.

Four black students trespassed a segregated lunch counter. One was interviewed. I often saw Alabama preachers interviewed and had viewed King looking angry in TV clips, along with photos of "rabble rousing" he led. Little of it made sense. This, however, did. The young man interviewed was a college student like me, a stack of textbooks like mine on the counter. Though broadcast on world news, he was only thirty miles away. I will never forget his words. He said he could shop every counter in downtown Greensboro except the lunch counter. When he got hungry he had to leave town to get food. He said, "That isn't fair!"

I had two and a half years of what would be an interminable higher education behind me, and had begun to peel back thick crusts of church-bound, Bible-based ignorance. But I swear, "That isn't fair!" which I'd first gleaned from Charlie about the no-dancing rule, was the first I'd heard from the rabble-roused black South that I could understand. It sounded like a revelation from God.

Although six years into it, I had not yet heard the term "Civil Rights Movement," and the term "Sit-in" would not be invented for a few weeks. Something irrevocable happened in my power-shrunk soul that night, and the soul of the nation. By the following fall I would have a new totem, enhanced spiritual power, and not a single lunch counter would be left legally segregated.

Next morning we talked about the Greensboro event in Dr. Murphy's Philosophy class, a discussion which merged moral thought with philosophical ethics, something new to me. I was confused and sleep-deprived, but now I was thinking. Three weeks later, February 23, 1960, it happened. (Ironically, this date was also the birthday, of Carol Wagster whom I'd yet to meet, but who in two years would be my wife, and who in a double irony was brought into the world eighteen years earlier to the day by a Tennessee obstetrician named George Williamson.) On that day, I spied a Philosophy classmate in anomalous coat and tie and asked, "What's up?" He and some others, through the briar patch of segregation, had made contact with students at the local black college to concoct a Greensboro-like event.

"Wanna go?" he asked.

"Why the hell not?"

I had been experimenting with my mischievous side. Many an evening Clough and I scaled past the NO TRESPASSING sign to the water tower catwalk or the forbidden library roof. I burned a dead squirrel under one fellow's dorm room door, scorching (and having to replace) the door, and led a portage of Ashley Hogewood's TR-3 into the narrow dorm hallway. Hog, we called him, the unlikeliest candidate, was soon to become my brother-in-law.

These were the years of phone-booth-stuffing and panty-raids. Trespassing Woolworth's struck me as one of those. Clad in a hastily donned jacket and crookedly knotted tie, I piled in the car and we were off, abuzz. Halfway there, what I was about to do struck with the force of a typhoon. Commit civil disobedience? No. I had never heard of civil disobedience. I was about to meet my first black peer.

CRIMINAL TRESPASS

I knew hundreds of black people, "the help" who waited on us, "knew" being a euphemism. It was one-sided acquaintance. They mostly struck me as scruffy, happy-go-lucky, cloudy of eye, but warm and affectionate, at least until rabble-rousing poisoned the atmosphere. I "knew" them only by first or nicknames, did not consider that they had family names—or families. And they were adults.

By contrast, the Greensboro Four were kids like me, college students who had textbooks—peers. The one interviewed wore glasses and spoke with a polished clip. The thought of imminently meeting such a person, accompanying him to a forbidden lunch counter, plunged me into panic, but before I could reconsider or take stock, there they were. There he was, the awesome racial other with whom I was partnered to sit at the counter: Skeet Diggs. Formally, his name was Jefferson Davis Diggs, though I didn't catch his name until four decades later when the colleges and the city invited us back to commemorate the sit-in.

We met, paired up, and headed for Woolworth's. I was struck dumb, clawing my mind for something, anything to say to nameless Skeet Diggs. After an eternity I snatched what frat boys regularly said in those racially charged days, my swaggering, "Whaddaya think of Martin Luther King!" In its 1960 Sigma Chi formulation, it was not a question, but a sneer-delivered fishing expedition, a friendly opening for a fellow frat boy to exhibit his best frat-cool vilification. I immediately learned that Skeet and I knew two different Martin Luther Kings. Mine was borne by the Sin I was born in, a Deep South caricature, disgust on Daddy's face, shudder in Kitty's slur, derision and rumbling in the cacophony of Buckhead banter. For Skeet, Martin Luther King was all Grace.

His response shamed me: a life testimony, a more fulsome expression of admiration and appreciation than I'd heard from or felt for anybody. I returned to mute, but his emotional affirmation began a slow dismantling of the kudzu thicket entangling my perceptions—after fifty years still underway. In my fading memory, I search for some moral or spiritual foothold by which I might have begun earlier recovery. But such a thing, for the life of me, I cannot find.

We entered Woolworth's. Before making it to the lunch counter, the manager precipitously closed the store and ushered everyone out. Suddenly Skeet and I were in this together, hurled beyond otherness by surprising success. We'd closed down a mighty Woolworth's. There was another Woolworth's, and in a rush of confident joy, we fairly danced the three blocks. At that one, however, the police, who until that moment I'd thought of as our "friends" ("the traffic safety people"), crisply surrounded us as we entered.

The best-decorated grimly identified himself. "I'm Chief Waller," he said, striking the first blow of my undoing. Nanny! My saintly, surpassingly jolly Tennessee grandmother, on hearing I would go to Wake Forest exclaimed that her friend Effie Waller's boy was police chief over there and I should meet him, an injunction I got on intervening visits and responded to with insincere assurances. Well, here Chief Waller was, along with my heritage and beloved family. I, however, was arm in arm, not with Nanny and family but with Jefferson Davis Diggs, the ultimate rabble-rousing other. Lost I was. Chief Waller said we had one minute to leave or we'd be arrested for something he ominously intoned, "criminal trespass."

Jim Crow, Baptist White Boy

I was paralyzed by the Chief's announcement. A few white boys slunk off. Skeet and his warriors, of course, were rooted there. I neither left nor stayed, just remained, de facto. Slowly passing seconds, after an eternity, struck sixty. Thereupon we were ceremoniously ushered out of an establishment which "reserved," as the sign said, and was legally granted, "the right to refuse service to anyone."

Stumbling altogether undone into the sunshine of that Dixie sidewalk, I saw them: family, church, fraternity, faculty, student body, an entire, tragic detritus of the cause long lost at Appomattox. They were there, clench-fisted, hurling soul-defiling obscenities—not at Skeet, it seemed to me, but at my traitorous Jim Crow, Baptist, whiteboy self! I saw it, the visage of a ghastly demon, lodged in the heart of my people.

We had only "known" each other for twenty minutes, but Skeet and I were suddenly wrenched apart by the arm of the law. We were cuffed in "separate but equal" paddy wagons, and whisked to "separate but equal" cells in the city jail. Mine had three drunks, four cots and a naked toilet. I was "ARRESTED," a new unwanted totem—along with three other names. One wouldn't exist for a few weeks until, at one of thousands to rage like a wildfire across Dixie, a journalist would invent "SIT-IN." A second I'd never heard, given the sheltered conventionality of my life, and wouldn't know until another day when a beloved professor would teach it to me: "CIVIL DISOBEDIENCE." Third was "NIGGER LOVER." Along with fellow white arrestees, I was a "Nigger Lover." I'd heard of such disreputables, but until I was one myself never actually met one. I was an alien. It was as if I had emigrated to a foreign country. I didn't know the language or landmarks. I couldn't imagine what I'd say to all the people I'd left behind.

We had separate but equal trials. The lawyer plead nolo contendere, a term from Roman legalese meaning "I contend nothing," in other words I did or didn't do it. The prosecutor, assisted by J. Edgar Hoover, alleged that Margaret Dutton, a fellow white criminal was sighted at a Communist rally while she was in Belgium the previous summer.

"Communists!" the next day's paper said, not just of Margaret, but of us all. "GUILTY," the judge shouted and whacked his mallet, of "nothing contended," a depressing anticlimax. At that agonizing moment in my twenty-year life, when I realized I knew almost nothing of consequential reality, I was awash in the existential conviction that quite apart from having broken somebody's so-called law, I really was guilty.

I didn't tell my parents, but we were in papers across the South, including theirs. They called, mortally upset, invited me home, and I went. Being heavy into repression, we somehow managed to get through the weekend without mentioning my cataclysm or the infinitely greater one descending on our culture.

What happened that day came to define who I am. Suddenly nineteen others and I were part of the still potential Sit-In Movement—its second public arrests. We were the new decade's second Civil Rights arrests, the Carolina Movement's first white arrests. Arrests were Non-violence's sine qua non. What we didn't really mean to do but were seduced by the Movement to do, was seized by social process and set into preordained slots in its symbol economy. To wit: idealistic youths jailed for an innocent act of fairness fatefully helped to discredit Segregation before the world. And ten white kids violated its most sacred taboo, publicly aided and abetted its dreaded enemy, and went over to the other side.

And something else, though I wouldn't realize it for a long time: this guilty, Southern whiteboy, Born in Sin and born Born Again, was Born Again, again.

DIVINE CACKLE

After the sit-in, Mac, my Christian Ethics professor, was the only person I could think of for guidance. Although I had only faint glimpse into his spirit, I liked him quite a lot. A campus character, his radicalism was fun to watch.

Mac spoke of South African Apartheid five years before Nelson Mandela went to prison. He lectured about colonialism's decay and nascent movements toward nationhood, as well as Clarence Jordan and his interracial Koinonia Farm in Georgia— where the new world coming thrived two decades in the very belly of the Beast. He introduced me to a prophetic understanding of Scripture.

Until I was in the Winston-Salem city jail, however, I didn't consider him an influence or register the significance of his teaching. In that dark night of my soul it slowly dawned that Mac's ideas, his radicalism, had taken root. What I wouldn't process until the fortieth anniversary of the Sit-in, celebrated by Wake and Winston-Salem State, was that all ten of the Wake sit-inners were Mac's students.

I went to see Mac as soon as I was released from jail. He told me what Civil Disobedience is, that what we'd done had been done before—forever. The rage hurled at us, he said, was the death throes of a still thriving Evil, that violation of unjust laws has regularly transformed history. He said Dr. King's "Movement" gave our little adventure a context which might propel it to historic significance, and that what we attempted is precisely what the Bible is about.

Over the next half-century I would complicate that insight, but in the spring of 1960 it's what I was ready for. Mac insisted that Hebrew Prophets aren't decorations for the Christmas story and Jesus isn't an icon snatching me from Hell. The Prophets and Jesus are the seminal civil disobedients. The Crucifixion/Resurrection has its entire meaning in the smashing impact of their political radicalism. I didn't entirely get it, still don't, and am on a half-century pilgrimage toward an epiphany. But in the spring of 1960, in Mac's office and in his and Edna's living room, I was bowled over by the force of his words as I stumbled down a radically new path.

When Mac cackled at my fundamentalism Freshman year, I was hurt. What teacher laughs at students' beliefs, let alone with the shrill cry of a hen? He only laughed at me once. But he cackled at one or more morally deplorable matters every time I talked with him over subsequent decades. I laughed as well, tickled by his sense of humor. Way too many leftist fellow travelers are anguished hand-wringers, under seeming moral obligation to bewail the wretched state of things and fret about "what to do, what to do." Jeremiah's anguished complaint against God was "You have filled me with indignation" (the typical fate of prophets, says the comic satire, the Book of Jonah.) More than any prophet I've known, Mac, hardly a hand-wringer, was the essential cackler. The other friend with this bizarre trait, although he never knew or knew of Mac, was Cliff.

I've puzzled at Mac's cackling. He never said, but here's my best guess: Tragedy plus Grace equals Comedy. Any particular predicament is potentially solvable—appropriate for concerned strategizing, perhaps even hand-wringing, but not the Human Predicament. There's nothing to be done about it. It's simply there, tragic. But in the Reality of God it's of no final account—because of Grace. Though wretched, it's no big deal. Therefore, we aren't compelled to resolve or even fret the Human Predicament. It's universal, shared by all things human including the humanity of God. We're free to embrace the human, warts and all. God is. God and we are liberated to find the universal ironic, the comical, the amusing grotesque, and take healing relief in laughter. The Divine Cackle conveys Grace.

Mac said we had stumbled into the prophetic, as did Jeremiah and Isaiah. Amos came to it slowly, like me, as social injustice gradually revealed itself. Hosea became a prophet without realizing it or meaning to in the maelstrom of personal confusion—like me. I found it watching prophetic people in my path. When I read Amos I imagined Mac, skinny as a rail, railing against compromise or idolatrous distortions of God. I read Jeremiah hearing the huge voice of Carlyle Marney, a prophetic white Southern preacher who blasphemed everything holy in Jim Crow paradise and took me under his ample wing. I saw Dan and Phil Berrigan in Jeremiah's outrageous street theatre, cursed by warmongers, condemned by powers, slapped in Jail. Isaiah, eloquent, courtly aristocratic, came alive when I heard Bill Coffin preach at Yale's Battell Chapel and quote Psalms at anti-war rallies, Bill the New England Aristocrat with a silver tongue. Bob Dylan's protest songs and gravelly voice was Hosea the bard singing sad songs of betrayal. Later I ran afoul of a Feminist Sunday School Class, irascible feminist modern-day versions of Amos; outrageous street theatre Jeremiahs; lofty, elegant, eloquent Isaiahs; sad, poetic, guitar-strumming Hoseas.

The prophetic proclaims to complacent publics and oppressive powers troubling truths that none of them want to hear. Mac enumerated countless movements before ours: Satiagrahis, Labor, the Irish Rising, Suffrage, Prohibition, Paris Commune, Abolition, French and American Revolutions, the Reformation, Friars Minor, the Jesus Movement, Hebrew Prophetic Movements and the Exodus. All gave their tithe to make me up. I refer to them as "THE GREAT ONES," but not in my memory. Memory began with Rosa Parks, the Bus Boycott, Dexter, Ebenezer and Sixteenth Street Churches, Sit-ins, SCLC, SNCC, Mississippi voter registration, Mississippi Freedom Democratic Party, Selma, Chicago Riots and the Garbage Workers' Strike. Before these, I was one thing; afterward, I was something else altogether. Taylor Branch, fellow Atlantan, won a Pulitzer claiming *The King Years,* 1954-68 redirected world history—not just me.

Two decades later in Uppsala, Sweden, strolling down a divided boulevard, I spied in the median a block away a striking sculpture. Two giant hands bent back a pair of jail bars. Approaching, I saw its inscription: "Martin Luther King."

I didn't see Skeet again for forty years, until "the multitude," in J.R. Lowell's apt phrase, had made "virtue of the truth they had denied" and transformed us into heroes. Had I simply crossed town and made friends with him, I would have saved a passel of heartache. What steps I took toward recovery were exhausting and shameful. I had no idea what I was doing. All the truths I had yet to discover were overwhelming: the history of Africa, the slave trade, the reality of slavery, Reconstruction; rudiments of social science; racism in the Bible, church history, colonialism, the Great Chain of Being; and the writings of Dr. King. Also I had to relearn the Bible I had already half-memorized, and unlearn a gaggle of hymns I knew by heart. And I hung out with Mac Bryan.

What in the Hell Happened to Us?

When it devoured us, "the Civil Rights Movement" hadn't officially happened yet. The March on Washington, its breakout on the world stage, was three years hence, and the Selma March, its signature moment, five. The Bus Boycott was five years past and King was not currently in the news. Black servants were still assuring white employers they didn't like him. Ebenezer and the other churches had been thrown out of their National Baptist Convention for "political activism." I assumed it was over. Until the Sit-ins, movement leaders were debating what, if anything, to do next.

After our arrests, King praised "the North Carolina students." In my racism I was humiliated. My fear, largely borne out, was that it would be assumed he'd organized us, or that we'd been his dupes. My column that week still resides like a burning coal of shame in the archives of Wake Forest: a tortuously ignorant and disingenuous disclaimer. I alleged, in good if misguided faith, that what we'd done had nothing whatsoever to do with King.

Of course, it had everything to do with King. With Rosa Parks' arrest, the Montgomery Improvement Association seized the day, converting the churches to dynamos of organization and inspiration. The black community experienced a once-a-generation fusion of passion and purpose. Newly invented television broadcasts elicited worldwide affirmation. Because the Movement lasted an entire year; because Martin Luther King, recently minted from theological education, got his voice, gathering into it the suppressed aspirations of his people; the Alabama event sparked a flame in millions of black people, readying them for revolution. By February 1960, it was just a matter of time.

What Ms. Parks did had been done many times across the South to no effect, but had stocked a waiting powder-keg of poised potential. Thousands of black subversions, unreported in white media, were the stuff of legend in black families and ghettos, a secret spirit of resistance. *Brown v. Board of Education* had flung wide the door to change. King's eloquent genius had erupted, like Gandhi's, as the eye of a gathering storm. And television's non-Southern journalists made The Movement visual to the nation. People instantly saw what transpired, an example and proven strategy to seize, motivating, among many others, the ten black students from Winston-Salem.

Montgomery also readied us ten white students. *Brown v. Board of Education* shattered the inevitability of segregation. Montgomery's tactic, persistent nonviolent subversive action, seized the common mind, establishing its idealism among liberals. Humanities classes even in Dixie gave it positive ethical analysis. The Greensboro Four Students captured imaginations of white students, adolescents in life-task rebellion against parents' culture and identity, organized in college communities across the south with non-Southern peers. Over the ensuing half-year, similar demonstrations happened spontaneously in hundreds of southern towns.

The yet-to-be-named Civil Rights Movement swept us ten white students into its wake, propelling us into the yet-to-be-named sit-ins. I was the lone frat boy among the ten, the other nine being "independents," unfettered by conservative lockstep of the fraternity system. All were influenced by Mac and by his affirmation of King and Montgomery. Five were Yankees, innocent of Jim Crow brainwash. Because we were shaped by the yet-unnamed Movement and surrounded by black colleagues who were the Movement's genuine children, when charged by cops either to commit Civil Disobedience or back down, we virtually had to do it.

But why didn't I repent of it? Family, friends, and nearly all my teachers shamed me with shunning, incredulity and white-hot racist rage. I got a night-long, tear-streaked grilling from the fraternity brother faculty member I loved most. Over the years I've been asked a thousand times what it was in me, my background, my makeup that accounts for this astonishing overhaul in my being, and have puzzled the matter ad nauseam. Here's my best guess.

What in the Hell Happened to Me?

It began with the Totem factor. For three years I wore the Not-Dancing-for-God symbol, a blatantly incongruous emblem for the world to see that I was God's kid. But then I was shorn of it, and like Samson absent his mane, I was drained of power, identity seeping from my core.

But amid the negative feedback flung at me after the Sit-in came a glimmer of respect, perhaps even awe, a reflected suspicion that I'd been taken up in something with transcendental implications. I'd acquired, quite accidentally, a new and more profound Totem.

There was Daddy's integrity. My Williamson grandparents possessed an ironclad commitment to principle that Daddy inherited whole-hog, but bore more graciously. For many years, more than anything, I wanted to be like him. I witnessed with pride the obvious admiration in which he was held at church—even by my clueless, adolescent friends. Perhaps even more fatefully, I observed in Herman Lay what I interpreted as moral reliance on Daddy's integrity, an aspect of Herman's fabulous success. Upended, I would begin to separate from the particulars of Daddy's morality, but the fact of it formed me.

Also, Kitty and Nanny. For the eleven years of Granddaddy's ordeal, Nanny and the Pearls tended his every need. Nanny spent only three nights away, when our family persuaded her to vacation with us. We still treasure a photo from then: a sassy, fleshy, cheesecake of her, hip sexily cocked. Kitty implanted in me her admiration for Nanny's storied selflessness, legendary in her Nashville circles, through her tears, and in substantial fact emulated. This, alongside Daddy's moral force, was a pole toward which my passions pointed.

And, of course, Mac's cackling influence.

Exiting Woolworth for the paddy wagon, I saw firsthand, inescapably and up close, the Demonic in the Old South reality I'd so innocently inhabited. There was Ralph McGill's soaring column; Eddie Mims, eating away at the foundations of my prejudices; the moral witness of the two Pearls. There was Cliff and Jesus. With Cliff I'd learned the snatches and wiggles of trying Jesus on for fit. For reasons I couldn't yet articulate, the Sit-in came to feel like a Jesus impersonation.

And the Bible. I endured forty years of ambiguity about the Bible before I was fully able to own it as integral to that week's inspiration—a story to come. Within twenty-four hours of being busted, I was talking to Mac about the Bible, specifically the Hebrew Prophets. I didn't know what he awakened. But I knew by heart from Hilda competitions the words "Do justice, love mercy, walk humbly with your God" and "Let justice roll down ...." I brought love and reverence for Scripture to our conversation, and though naïve and twisted, comprehensive knowledge of it. Suddenly, having understood it one way, I was shaken with news of another, perhaps uniquely authentic way.

The Bus Boycott was churches, prophetic religion, passions of spiritual *ekstasis* and self-sacrificing discipline of religious community. Such religion or its secular facsimile is the heart of every social movement. But the Sit-ins added students. Students live by ideas more than any other social group. They have unique access and susceptibility to revolutionary propaganda. Adolescent students are rebellious by life-task, unrestricted by tradition and social formation, emotionally volatile, free of binding commitments, luxurious with energy and time, organized in schools, and in company with revolutionaries like the young Moses, Jeremiah, the "twelve disciples," Luther, Jefferson, LaFayette, Michael Collins. In 1960 the baton passed from black churches to black schools, and most importantly to Fisk University, the Movement's truest radicals. Perhaps the most significant result of the Sit-ins was the birth at Fisk of the Student Nonviolent Coordinating Committee, to radicalize the conservative Southern Christian Leadership Conference.

None of this was apparent on February 23, 1960, when my

buddies and I left campus for reckless adventure. At least I went without awareness. We had free will and some intentionality. But a complex social-historical dynamic, ballooning immensely beyond our sight, silently drew and motivated us, set and then restricted our choices, defined the significance of what we did, took things entirely from our hands. We were part of something invisible that would make and redirect History, and redefine who we were.

It transformed my moral essence, infused me with energy and redirected my life. Nearly everything about me came radically into question. I was virtually cut off from Dixie, flung into the chaos of galloping, deconstructed History, with emerging History my means of reconstruction.

It was traumatic in the extreme, but morally good, a renewed identity, an unimagined but redemptive destiny I couldn't have found any other way. I was a reborn child of The Movement. Grace.

Georgia friends heard about the sit-in and sent a framed drawing of me sitting at a counter with four black men. They were caricatured "pictures of the enemy:" snaggle-toothed, huge floppy lips, low, simian back-slanted foreheads, cumbersome jaws, clad in overalls, flies buzzing about their heads. All were pounding my back in apparent congratulation with big gnarled hands. I received it with ironic pride, and with knowing laughter regularly displayed it, as if to say, "Not, of course, my attitude, but it is funny, isn't it?"

My mostly unsuccessful quest for an unfound curriculum took grueling years of further education. I didn't know what I didn't know, or that I didn't know. I needed relationships to black people, swapped home visits, shared crises, confrontive racism workshops, spiritual disciplines of repentance and reconciliation; to know myself and all I didn't want to know. For fifty years I stumbled these steps down a dark pilgrimage of shame, self-doubt and loneliness, toward recovery.

What a waste. How much could I have accomplished had I simply driven over and made friends with Skeet? What I did instead was to massively redirect my life, and to fall in love with Carol Wagster.

Becoming Someone Else

At some foggy point it became clear I couldn't grow up to be a preacher like Dr. Swilley. Rather than abandon the profession altogether, I concocted a more treacherous alternative. Dr. Swilley, Second-Ponce de Leon, Southern Baptists, the Bible and Jesus of my sylvan walks had conspired to make me a racist, anti-intellectual, worldly ignoramus, alien to literature and world affairs. It wasn't enough to abandon their imposed destiny.

Upended from Baptist Heaven to material earth, I set out to upend them. I decided not to go to Southern Baptist Seminary like Dr. Swilley. Instead, I bussed to New Haven to explore Yale Divinity School, bastion of academic religion, intellectual birthplace of Mac Bryan. In a seedy New Haven YMCA, sleeping on a lumpy cot with dirty sheets, I had a nightmare. Heaven appeared, shiny, ethereal: Southern Baptist Seminary. And Hell, reeking of sulfur: Yale. In fact, when I mounted the hill and took a look, Yale looked like Thomas Jefferson's idyllic quadrangle at the University of Virginia—his paradise.

I spent three years there, meeting the wide world, acquiring an air of supercilious superiority to my heritage, and despite all, becoming my old destiny: a Southern Baptist preacher. Cliff was at Yale, studying Political Science. Having been upended, I plunged headlong into the scientific study of the Bible, falling ever farther from the kid I had been. I had Cliff to laugh with about it, so I didn't fall so far.

Actually, I fall a lot. On a spring day in 1962, two months before I was plighted to marry beautiful Carol, some friends and I abandoned the library for the Connecticut landscape. We trekked to Sleeping Giant, a hauntingly eerie mountain which strikingly resembles a reclining giant man. The fateful catastrophe is buried beneath an abyss of traumatic amnesia, troubled only by the occasional flicker of fragmented memory. But I'm told that on mounting the giant's face and nose, I, the climbing daredevil of Buckhead, started down the sheer cliff of his chin. I fell. On subsequent reconnaissance, the fall looked to have been about forty feet. I landed on my face. The square of earth I crashed on was nestled between boulders. A sign just there read, "No Climbing on Cliff." According to the *New Haven Register*, my companions rounded up hikers and passed me down the giant's shoulders, whence I was whisked to Yale - New Haven Hospital.

Medical records say I bled thirteen pints (about my capacity) ballooning my face like the Goodyear Blimp. An overqualified surgeon, licensed in dentistry, dental surgery, internal medicine, and plastic surgery, massively rearranged the crushed facial structure under the swollen skin. I was his first, possibly only patient to challenge such oddly assembled skills. He'd been headed out the door for extended vacation when they called. Canceling the vacation, working long-handle tools through slits beneath eye and chin, he restored dislodged teeth, wired my jaw and sinus bones. He later showed slides to the New England Medical Association, then brought me out for a standing ovation. Happily, I was spared seeing the slides, except a gigantic close-up of the multicolored blimp.

I was mostly unconscious two weeks. I awoke with a fateful stretch of life deleted from mind, mouth wired shut, a hole from two missing front teeth accommodating a straw for sucking liquefied food, a tracheotomy for breathing, a multi-hued discoloration of visage to strike dread in passersby, vessels full of someone else's blood, and a new face I didn't recognize. After fifty-odd years mirrors shock me still. I crawled back to school and got hauled down to Columbia, Tennessee ("Mule Town, USA") and, given Carol's ill-advised willingness, got married anyway.

While I was in the hospital, William Faulkner died, as did the two most prominent theologians at Yale Divinity School, two of America's most prominent: Robert Lowry Calhoun and H. Richard Niebuhr. And Carol's grandfather died.

By the fall of 1960, despite sit-in and jail, I was still a Republican—because of Daddy. Wake had a mock vote, Kennedy vs. Nixon, and I accepted an invitation to speak for Nixon before the student body. I said Kennedy was a Communist, that given his Catholicism the Pope would take over the country, which is what Daddy said. I embarrassed myself. My opponent, head of Young Democrats, went on to a political career. He knew his stuff and not only demolished, but also convinced me. I did win the debate, and Nixon the vote, but I began reading about JFK and actually cast my first vote for him. His campaign was something of a social movement among enthusiastic Democrats, and once again I got caught up. His election and early Camelot days were thrilling for Carol and me.

That summer I took an internship in Dallas, where my parents had moved, and enjoyed Carol's integration into our family. The church was massive, pure Texas, having grown under the same pastor from nothing to huge in two decades. It still sported the motto of its origins, "Where everybody is somebody," "everybody" being a euphemism like "All men are created equal." By the time I got there the motto was an ironic self-mockery. Among its thousands, "everybody" was really "somebody": big-talking, rich, "love Dallas, don't you?" I hated Dallas. I never encountered anyone there who didn't hate Dr. King and President Kennedy. Eighty-three days after returning to New Haven, I was lying on a cot in the Yale gym giving blood. Someone screamed into the gym that President Kennedy had been shot—in Dallas.

Carol and I sat with our friends in the dorm TV room watching the unfolding horror of those unspeakable events, everyone weeping. There had been "Kennedy Traitor: Wanted Dead or Alive" leaflets in Dallas. Children in schools cheered at his death. The memorial service in Marquand Chapel at Yale was profound and shaped my commitment to ritual. I first heard and sang there what would become my favorite Easter hymn, "The strife is o'er, the battle won, the victory of life is done, the song of triumph has begun, Alleluia."

What I didn't Learn at Yale

Three years of Yale were a massive challenge for a provincial, congenital anti-intellectual. I caught whiffs from the fading charisma of the Neo-Orthodox movement in theology. I heard from the last words of H. Richard Niebuhr and Robert Lowry Calhoun. I snatched the social ethics mantle laid on my slender shoulders by Mac Bryan, and began serious study with young Jim Gustafson who was destined for super-stardom in the field. I learned, tortuously, how to read, and began a lifelong adventure in biblical scholarship. I got from Jim Dittes a useful introduction to pastoral care, which would consume probably the largest number of hours in the profession I was soon to enter. Just being at Yale jerked me all the way around from my natal identity.

"Clinical pastoral training," by now a staple in seminary education, was then a new experimental venture with only two fledgling programs in the country. Ironically, one was at Wake Forest. As Carol was still working on her degree from Wake, we went there for the summer. We had been there the summer before, when I interned in a church, discovering some unhappy things about myself. My boss, Richard Hannah, a gifted Christian Educator, was killed in a horribly tragic automobile accident in Mexico. Four church kids, my alleged charges, on a work trip with him were also killed. I was too terrified to speak with their families and the other church kids, incapable of effective ministry to them. Clinical training in the same city was to be my solution.

The program was run by Dick Young, a pioneer in the field. We had hospital chaplaincy duties. We gave verbatim accounts of interactions with patients in daily encounter sessions with Dick. He turned us merciless with each other in evaluations. The goal was to find what was rumbling in ourselves as we listened to people in crises, and learn what to do with it. I felt the critical feedback I gave was first rate, was rather proud of myself. Whereas others were regularly reduced to tears, I came sailing through, reveling in the whole thing.

At the end, Dick confronted each with critiques of weaknesses and kudos for strengths. Last, he came to me, happily expectant of praise for my sparkling insights. He said, "And, Williamson. Williamson, you wasted the summer. You never revealed a single thing about yourself."

Carol, who showed only sweetness and warmth during our brief, mostly long-distance courtship, was much more volatile and confrontive than I in daily life and had passionate, often angry exchanges with her family, which I found off the charts compared to our Williamson repressions. When she turned her Wagster furies toward me, I withdrew into cocoons of emotionless passive aggression. She responded by saying I hadn't a clue about myself.

She was now confirmed by the expert.

That was the summit of my Yale education, though, ironically, it happened back at Wake. I learned nothing at Yale about social action, which was to be the notorious heart of my ministry. That was my fault, not Yale's. Bill Coffin, the Yale Chaplain, was a Freedom Rider, and could have taught me much. He brought Dr. King to campus—my surviving racism found him too "black-preacher" for my new Yale intellectualism. Bill, whom I wouldn't know until I was a chaplaincy colleague two decades later, was early to organize students to lobby and demonstrate against US involvement in Vietnam. Still reeling from the trauma of the sit-in, I wasn't yet into that, so missed it all.

I learned nothing at Yale about preaching, though preacher is what I would be. The only course I ever flunked was public speaking, and what I learned in homiletics (preaching) class was irrelevant to the preaching I'd actually do, though Yale did award me its preaching prize. I learned nothing about church administration, chief among many failures. I got fired from my first field work for sophomoric radicalism, nearly fired from my second for drinking alcohol, which I'd only just taken up, faired indifferently in two more, and got no meaningful supervision.

My favorite Yale story is of Robert Calhoun, then America's

most revered historical theologian. From humbler stock than Yale, he'd don overalls and deliver eggs from his chickens to neighbors. They knew him as "Bob the egg man." One day his dressed-up customer said he was going to hear the famous theologian Paul Tillich at Yale. Bob the egg man astonished the customer by asking if he could go with him. After the lecture Bob stood in his overalls. His host gasped. Tillich said, "Yes Bob?" And Bob the egg man roundly critiqued the great man with citations from the history of theology. That gave me a model for the sort of character I might want to be. In truth, by the time I graduated, I didn't know enough to be that or anything else worth a damn.

PROFESSIONAL HOLY MAN

My first post after graduation was a "two-church field," a rural outpost of northern Virginia piety that involved two churches linked together. One was Appalachian, a new and refreshing culture for us; the other, with suburban pretensions, older Olde South even than Buckhead. I would make a mad dash, leaving one church as it began its closing hymn, rushing in the door of the other singing "Amen" to its opening hymn.

We lived above a leading family's rank two-hundred-cow dairy barn. The owner had reputedly been Ku Klux Klan, the other farmers there were pure Jim Crow. We enjoyed three years in splendid shadows of the Blue Ridge, acquired Duchess, our first German Shepherd, and stuffed our souls with scenery and stomachs with country cooking (the first ten of my adult forty pounds). The Civil Rights Movement coincidentally arrived with us. I tried Movement preaching and organizing, accomplished nothing, got all but fired, and learned how much I hadn't learned at Yale.

I wasn't there two days, still damp from seminary, still eager, when I received a late evening phone call from a police chief whom I didn't know. He informed me, not yet a pastor, that I was pastor of a widow, whom I didn't know either, whose only son had just died in a car wreck. I must go with him to break the news. We met on a nighttime road—police official and official holy man. His menacing cruiser led the way on a pitch-dark unpaved lane with no houses, down a rutted wooded drive to a tiny, peeling, sad and seedy cabin. He officially conveyed the unspeakable to the mother and drove off, leaving us alone. Alone. I do not remember what I said— probably everything I'd learned in seminary, its taste gushing over my tongue as of a pack of lies. Forty years later, preaching on the words of Jesus, "My God, why have you forsaken me?" I thought of her. I wished I'd told her that Jesus, nearly dead, cried this bitter rhetorical question and, like her, got no answer either.

What I did learn at Yale—if not profundities of theological insight—was sociology and psychology of religion from Gustafson and Dittes. I had no theological imperatives to propel Virginia farmers from Jim Crow to discipleship, but I did have social science about my job's structure and function. Leaving the godforsaken widow, it clobbered me. I was a professional holy man.

My structure was the mundane religious institution, not the divinity enthusiast's Kingdom of God. My function, the religious function, was not to make authentic disciples, but to administer religious consolation. A scant hour on the job and I'd already failed. Encountering the widow was my initial awakening that the religious function and holy man role is intrinsic to human existence. Whatever prophetic witness I might have to offer my parishioners, they had a passel of non-negotiable needs that I as their pastor had damn well better answer to—a dread fact I would puzzle over for all the decades to come.

I DIDN'T KNOW NEARLY ENOUGH

In Virginia I stumbled down the knife-edge between role and calling, fulfilling neither. I wasn't fired, but indelible handwriting was all over the wall. Truth is, I didn't know enough: not nearly enough about the social-psychological dynamics of my profession, the prophetic dynamics pulling against them, or my theology. So, after remedial reading, I got into a new PhD program in Christian Ethics at Vanderbilt—two students, three faculty.

By then, despite mounting failures, I'd done one thing right. Beginning with the Mac Bryan conversations following the sit-in, I'd fallen in love with Martin Luther King. Like millions of my generation, quite despite myself and altogether without intention, I was swept up in his charisma, acquired the biblical "ears to hear" and became a true believer. But just then, salt tears of conversion still damp on my cheeks, he betrayed me. He made war on The War.

Despite my affectation of the prophetic mantle, Vietnam hadn't caught my attention, overcrowded as it was with the jumbled chaos of race. It wasn't yet much of a war. I still indulged my cowboy-and-Indian, Bible-war-stories, Popo mode. Virginia congregants included veterans. My selective service classification was 4D ("D" for "Divinity") exempting me for my... divinity. Not expecting to serve, I did not give a second thought to war's morality. My passive thrill in and acquiescence to massive violence joined meaner, more aggressive enthusiasms of others: the gun and gun-killing frenzy of American culture, defense industry lobbyists, tail-wagging-the-dog political priorities, US geopolitical imperatives. The horror visited upon southeast Asians, on young Americans ruined by it, on the national psyche wouldn't have happened had it not been for this human predicament among the likes of me.

Opposition to the war had not gained much public attention by the time of Dr. King's great speech at Riverside Church. His outcry therefore clobbered me with an emotional tidal wave.

My new hero, without warning, forsook the still segregated, bitterly contested South, ascended the pulpit of a New York church, and from the headlines, preached against my country at war. He abandoned me, a fresh true-believer in what we'd begun to call a "Civil Rights Movement," and undermined American "boys," my peers, dying for my country. The first black ever to evoke political favor from a president cavalierly opposed Johnson's signature policy, squandering his benevolence. And he implicated me in his treason. What I read from the paper I heard from a chorus of King's seasoned black supporters: international fame had inflated his hubris into demagoguery. He imagined himself entitled to make headlines on whatever matter, however remote from his expertise. I'd been duped.

Nonetheless, from smoldering resistance such as I'd witnessed at Yale, the speech ignited a genuine anti-war movement. I didn't actually read his speech until I'd heard respected grad school colleagues mention its alleged brilliance. Having been wrong on one movement already, I reluctantly decided to check this one out. So I read it, about the moral failure of violence in international disputes, the distraction from higher moral priorities. He said there was a blatantly racist dimension—a disproportion of poor African-Americans sent half a world away to kill Asians for reasons opaque to them. My wake-up call.

So, I was Born Again yet again—antiwar: the feeling of being upended, uprooted from my origins and forcefully toppled, then set right side up by mysterious social forces. There was no devastating conversion as in my traumatic confrontation with race. The shame came slowly and took years, me still singing of rockets' red glare, bombs bursting in air, hand over heart, eyes moist.

About then I had my first encounter with the new Feminist Movement, the only discussion I remember in my allegedly liberal ethics program of "feminist issues." It concerned recent protests against college parietal hours for women, *in loco parentis.* (From the Latin derivative for "wall." The parietal system walled off males from female dorms.) Andie was my first feminist peer, and living with her boyfriend, the first "modern woman" of my acquaintance. She said the college scene was predatory to women. She said adolescent women were ill-equipped to handle it, that parietals were necessary for their protection. No one in class had read *The Feminine Mystique*, including Andie. There was the new term, "bra-burner," and modern Andie's revelation about the fragility of women. Given my origins, that was all I needed to know. And not know.

GRACE

If life were like corporate America, I'd have long since been fired. As a child, I had spectacular performance reviews from family, Sunday School and Dr. Swilley. Hilda's mother hoped we'd marry, joined forever on the front pew. I was so far a moral superstar, spiritual prodigy, one hell of a dude. But then came a disastrous racist evaluation to clobber my confidence, followed by a quick succession of shameful messages that my race performance was by no means the worst of it. Not just me, of course. It was us, together. It's been fifty years since management gave me a good assessment, while an out-of-the-blue series of negative feedbacks, any one of which would have sunk a promising corporate career, have been relentless.

I had five memorable moments in my time at Vanderbilt.

First, slumped in my carrel deep in library stacks, I was reading Tillich, the most intellectual of theologians, slogging through, sentence by obtuse sentence, like my hundred pages of *Moby Dick*. Hardier now, more ascetic, I toughed it out, picked up speed, scribbled pages of notes. Suddenly it struck in a rush of ambiguous feeling that I, Bible-stuffed ignoramus from Buckhead, understood Tillich! Thrilling, but not simply, it was my culmination of disenchantment. I'd scaled new heights, new vistas ahead, but receding behind was a vast continent of self, lost. Wordsworth said, "The things that I have seen, I now can see no more."

Second was my first experience as a teacher. I was researching Reinhold Niebuhr's Christian Realism for my dissertation, yet I was also awakening to the new radicalism on campuses of which Realists were contemptuous. So when offered a chance to teach, I decided to explore the new Spirit as an ethical alternative to Realism. I called it "Radical Politics and Conscience," opening what for four decades would be a primary intellectual engagement.

The other three moments came in quick succession. Dr. King

was assassinated in Memphis. The next day I went (outsider white guy) to an infinite landscape of black mourners, silent as sentinels, reliving three centuries come to inevitable conclusion; then went back, dazed and disillusioned. Nashville, like a Third World capital, was occupied by the Tennessee National Guard. Tanks and helmeted warriors patrolled the streets, cannons aimed at the city from Capitol Hill.

While the National Guard occupied Nashville, word got out that I had an association with the Lay company. Since the private wealth and public influence of a leading banker in the area came largely from his investments with Herman Lay, I was dispatched to the great man to enlist his influence for removal of the occupation.

The paneled confines of his imposing throne room high above Middle Tennessee imprinted on my little mind as stage for my humiliation. He judged me for what in fact I was. Presumptuous. Hopelessly naïve. I, of course, accomplished precisely nothing.

Then, on a May day, a colleague called across a busy street, "Soldiers are shooting students at a college in Ohio." It was Kent State. Wordsworth again: "I know, where'er I go, that there has passed away a glory from the earth."

I eventually earned a PhD in ethics, certifying my expertise in matters of right and wrong, good and evil, duty, value, obligation, virtue and character. I learned enough about the moral issues overwhelming my life to pass exams and produce credible lectures and articles. Though wrenched about, I finally felt secure in my new identity as ethical guru, benevolently contemptuous of benighted souls who were still like I used to be.

A quick succession of traumatic conversions, still painful and confusing to recall, would soon upend my hard won confidence. I was awash in a spiritual reality which undermines divine Creation: Sin. Like many in my generation who share my experiences, this trajectory of disenchantment was tumbling toward a clichéd outcome, cynicism, but not for me. I had what tough-love advocates call an "intervention." My tangle in Sin was overturned by its opposite. Opposite is the Creation itself. But not this spoiled Creation. Nor is its opposite Jesus, the alleged good man. The opposite of Sin is Grace. Born, nourished, complicit and downright religious in Sin, having long since lost grasp and facility for Grace, Grace nonetheless came and got me. My adopted name is Grace.

Amazing Grace

Actually, my name is Butch. I was born "George" (Born in Sin "George"), what Kitty named me ("Jaw-idge"), what I go by. But Daddy "George" anointed me "Butch." "Butch" meant riding in the basket of Daddy's bike, going to his office on Saturdays, a warm and fuzzy secret me. Wob and Joe in the ivy patch behind our garage, "imaginary friends" presumptuously maligned by a shrink who didn't know them, called me "Butch." Popo, called "Porter" by everybody else, said "Butch-o" to rhyme with "Popo." And Bobby Reddy, Granddaddy's best friend who lived with Nanny and Granddaddy, a gift to me and my cousins, a non-related relative we got from nowhere. He built my big electric train layout with me. A former pitcher with the Macon, Georgia team, he taught me the curve ball. He and his dog, Pluto, who lived atop Nanny's basement stairs, were what I loved most at Nanny's. When Bobby called "Butch," it meant my time had come. Daddy's dead, Bobby's long dead, Popo just died in his nineties—the only one for decades who still called me "Butch(-o)," a fading echo of Grace.

From the front end of life until its finish, the moments that turn out to matter can be counted on the fingers and toes. For the most part you see them only in the rear-view mirror after they've lumbered by unnoticed, until the evidence of whatever's happening has accumulated. Finding apparently unrelated occurrences and stringing them into a story is the adventure of this memoir.

Jobs were scarce in 1970. I'd burned bridges with Southern Baptists and was unenthusiastic about academia. There was, however, an offer from a seminary in another denomination. Carol and I drove to check it out and decided to accept, though I deferred formal acceptance, still hoping for a church. When we arrived at home that night there was a telegram urging me to call Vassar College, a famous elitist women's college somewhere in the northeast. I called.

"Are you interested in the job?" somebody up there said.

"What job?' "College Chaplain and Assistant Professor of Religion." "Never heard of it. I'm about to take another position." "When?" "Monday." "Can you come here tomorrow?" "Tomorrow?" "We'll fly you." Why not?

At Vassar I found a group of black students blockading the president's office. They let me in. The president said, "On paper" (What paper?) "You're the leading candidate." Really? "But a decision will take weeks. Postpone your seminary offer," he said, dismissing my obligation and opportunity. Steamed at his presumption I refused, adding that if I were chaplain I'd be "sitting out there with the black students." I knew I was burning the Vassar bridge. Still, I kept a meeting with the student committee. They too knew stuff about me (How?) and seemed genuinely interested. I liked them a lot, but told them I hadn't considered chaplaincy, knew nothing about Vassar, was furious at the administration's arrogant assumption, and repeated my parting comment to the president. This turned out to be exactly what they were looking for. On the basis of my disinterest and irreverence they picked me. Student power being what it was I got the job before I left. I couldn't believe it. Making the trip with not a little bemusement, I was seduced by the kids. The day was pure thrill.

As my first Vassar stint I took students to a Yale retreat. For closing they sang "Amazing Grace." I offered to lead it. I knew it from singing with song leaders Sunday nights in Buckhead, led it myself as North Fulton Christian Fellowship song leader. Judy Collins' "Amazing Grace" was Number One on the pop charts. Students knew the first verse, but singing all four to rousing evangelical manipulation, they became a true-believer congregation in a charismatic moment. I was the coolest dude, knew the currentest of songs extracted from the with-it-est generation the decade's very sound, a rush to the ego. Actually, it's Baptist Hymnal #180. I was pure fraud.

My second task was joining college physicians in "the sex lecture" for freshmen, who in fact were the front end of the sexual revolution, many having just had their first "amazing grace" experience. I told them to go ahead—but be nice.

Third was the president's faculty reception. This was my initial encounter with new colleagues. Some were atheist, more anti-religious, many more Jewish, a lot vocally anti-chaplaincy, most grumbling at "a Southern Baptist" chaplain. The reception ended on the front porch, where faculty greeted the sprawled student body, fresh from their own reception.

A retreat kid spied me, called "George!" and "Amazing Grace!" which became a chant. The president, a reserved, dignified Brit, was perplexed, ditto my colleagues. Not me. To mounting chants I stepped forward and astonished the porch crowd by lining the words. I was accompanied by two thousand emotional voices, a swaying multitude, arms linked, rolling waves of testosterone and liquor fumes, another charismatic moment. "Amazing Grace" became as regular at college opening as the sex lecture, also at political rallies, even at occasional faculty parties. I did "Amazing Grace" at the president's retirement years later. Whatever I was in those days, I was the Amazing-Grace-guy.

In my Religion class I asked secular, with-it, born-again-Youth-Movement kids about "Amazing Grace." "Judy Collins wrote it," said Andy, yarmulke on his fuzz. They all agreed, except one student from Carol's Tennessee hometown who knew better. We showed them Baptist Hymnal #180. They were dumbfounded.

It was a movement song before a hymn: "Amazing Grace, how sweet the sound, that saved a wretch like me," composed by a slave trader on conversion from his trafficking by an Abolitionist preacher. "I once was lost, but now am found; was blind, but now I see. T'was Grace that taught my heart to fear, and Grace my fears relieved. How precious did that Grace appear the hour I first believed." These are lyrics of classic Born-Again conviction of the Evil done, conversion and ecstasy.

"Through many dangers, toils and snares, we have already come": Perils of uprising familiar to radicals. As is "'Twas Grace that brought us safe thus far, and Grace will lead us home" miraculous victory. Then the surpassing eschatological finale: "When we've been there ten thousand years, Bright shining as the sun, We've no less days to sing God's praise than when we first begun." This is the only allusion to God, for secularists a metaphor for a liberated society surely coming "someday."

No song (not "The Times, They Are a-Changin'," "Bridge over Troubled Waters" or "The Sound of Silence") so inspired and bore witness to the spirit of those emotional days. The wild enthusiasm of the Civil Rights Movement cruelly dashed, the song bore its spiritual fire among white, anti-cultural Student-Movement-kids. This was a decade after Grace taught my heart to fear at the sit-in, still searching for release from guilt, I adopted "Amazing Grace" as my new totem. How precious Grace appeared during that moment of many to come.

VASSAR AND SEXISM

Three months after meeting Search Committee students I was in the vast Vassar Chapel, robed in a role I hadn't applied or prepared for, no idea what I was doing. I preached, a frowning president and his wife on the front row. Afterward, at the faux-medieval front door, a fierce adolescent female told me, given my scripture, language and subject matter, I was a sexist pig.

Dr. King did not prepare me for this. Sojourner Truth, Harriet Tubman, even Rosa Parks, Fannie Lou Hamer or Coretta were not yet Movement icons. Women did not appear in classic Movement photos. The great shot of Rosa Parks next to a white man on the bus, staged later by a journalist, didn't exist yet. Heroic black women of course eventually found their voice, but not in Dr. King's time. J. Edgar Hoover, spying on King for propaganda, exposed his mistress, humiliating Coretta. He too was Born in Sin. My awakening didn't include women. I had not read a female in my field, just the one discussion with Andie of "feminist issues."

An angry student insisted I read Mary Daly's *Beyond God the Father.* Talk about jerked around! Here I was pastor, teacher of religion, practitioner of the cure of souls and preacher to young female proponents of a revolution. I did not have ears to hear. How could my student interviewers not have seen this?

They persuaded me to invite Mary Daly. Not to preach. That, I swear, did not occur, so alien was the concept of a female preacher. To lecture. I had to introduce her. A raging prophet against religion, Daly was my first feminist superstar. I was even more terrified of her than of Skeet. I should have confessed this, but I was too insecure. Defensive, shamed, grasping for familiar weapons, I learned nothing from her. In her wake, exhausted, I went home for a nap.

Students confronted my sexist language, predatory use of the masculine as if the feminine didn't exist. "He," "man," "sons," leapt out my mouth into the waiting contempt of every Vassar feminist. I remember successive emotional reactions, roughly Kubler-Ross' seven stages of grief. I made no real progress until the entire demonic structure began to be dismantled. At some level I passively presumed that we brothers inherited ontological primacy, that misogynist dismissal of the female in common language was inconsequential. My habit was a cover. With minimal positive and negative reinforcement, habit can be broken. Required was Exorcism.

Exorcism occurred in the context of three things: marriage to Carol, who took to Vassar feminism like a fish to water; parenting Chris, born at Vassar, born feminist, as if she'd suffered centuries of sexism in the womb; and friendships with graciously prophetic women. Examples are too painful to record. When Carol complained that I hadn't changed our new son's diaper I said, "That's not the kind of relationship with him I want to have." Carol's response was classic Hebrew Prophets. It took a while, but I came to be more ashamed of that statement than of any other single thing I ever said. Redemption is Exorcism.

I did not think of Vassar as one of the world's leading feminist institutions, nor did I imagine its newly coed feminism in crisis. The Seven College Conference ("Seven Sisters") to which Vassar belongs had "brother" Ivy League schools. Yielding to feminist attacks, Brothers admitted women and more intimately embraced their Sisters. But Vassar and its brother Yale were a hundred miles out of reach. Vassar considered moving in with Yale. The decision to become coed—alone among the Sisters—was the alternative. Hence the crisis. I arrived on what was being called "the Vassar experiment," admitting junior men, then when I arrived, "experimental" male freshmen.

The Feminist Movement, not yet in Virginia, was merely academic in grad school. Whereas I grew up across barricades from The Movement, feminism seemed silly to me. What was roaring like a hurricane through Vassar caught me unprepared. I had female superiors, seasoned feminists connected with Movement leadership. Most students were female, a minute minority of women who'd chosen a feminist institution to earn stripes in the struggle. More striking were males, a hundred-fifty among eighteen hundred assertive women. Talk about minute minorities! Of a million US freshman peers, they alone chose a feminist institution. More than the women, they knew exactly what they were doing. They knew more about feminism than many women and were urgent to display credentials. Classes were Vassar-experiment-labs. Feminist profs railed nourishing feminist consciousness and commitment: "Keep Vassar the best women's education" amid the threatening influx of testosterone. Restrain male dominance. Anecdotally at least, I was where the Feminist Movement was most overtly raging during 1970-71.

I learned about male chauvinist pigs—me. Humiliated and intimidated, as with Black kids who were in the Movement, I had years of catch-up, starting on the fly from scratch. But I loved and admired these women. They were committed to bring me along, and I was brought along by the best. Pointedly contemptuous of patriarchy in my mouth and on my person, they loved me, wanted me better, plotted my cure. Chapel Board was a workshop undoing millennia of religious patriarchy, creating redemptive transcendence for Movement folks. Then Chris was born. The delivery announcement should have been "It's a feminist!" Peter, Dan and me, now a minority of three in a feminist household of five.

The maelstrom of the Feminist Movement whirling down on me, I never got beyond range of Sisters' revolutionary rage or their signature broadside—"You just don't get it." Yet from then on I was in and of the movement, profoundly changed by it, meeting, marching, and crying out with Sisters, preaching and writing their themes, giving pastoral care to their wounds.

I was intensely transformed. But only when I moved to a Midwestern town where feminism was quiescent, to a church using sexist language, in a denomination rejecting female ordination, did I officially join the movement. Ordaining a dozen women (and two men), my mind, theology and direction were profoundly reformed—by a Sunday School class.

DRUGGED

In some ways the Sixties began in Nashville, before I got there, at the Nashville Sit-ins. Jim Lawson, Vanderbilt Divinity School's first black student had studied with Satyagrahis and brought Gandhi to the Movement even before King did. He was teaching non-violent resistance to Fisk students when Greensboro happened. He staged a sit-in, was arrested and expelled from Vanderbilt. The Divinity faculty resigned en masse, and he was readmitted. His Fisk followers went on to form SNCC, the Mississippi Voter Registration Project, and to become the Movement's left wing.

But that wasn't The Sixties. The Movement, poor, black and southern, was parent to The Sixties which was flower children at Columbia and Berkeley, affluent, white, California and East Coast. Black students, into Malcolm X, found me way too white. But white kids swept me into their movement—Amazing Grace—flipped me over again and cast me like dice, across the green felt gambling table of History. There was Sixties detritus in Nashville, but buried in grad school stacks. I didn't see it. My Sixties began in April, 1970, meeting the Vassar kids. They adopted me into their decade, which in 1970 according to their internal calendars, was only half done.

Pat Sullivan joined the Religion faculty when I did, his considerable charisma acquired in India studying Hinduism. Tall, lean, capped by a prematurely gray pageboy, he moved with silky grace and spoke in otherworldly eloquence of eastern spirituality. His students, true believers of those urgent days, were mine too. They echoed Pat, floating through my classes, trailing his aura. We were friends, and I envied him. A lapsed Catholic-Anglican priest, he sparkled with tough-minded, irreverent wit. In academic cant, he needled me ("the college reverend," "the religious one") by contrast to his implicitly superior "secularity." In fact, next to his spirituality, I was mundane, the secular one. Students really were secular, most with little exposure to religion, but with an influx of aspiration from the Movement, they were awakening to Eastern religion. Pat was their spiritual mentor. I was for radical politics.

When students sat-in over a student power issue, I imported a movement guru whose book was hot for a "Teach-in" at the sit-in. His shallow book, like most fierce, partisan, intellectualism of those days, spoke to us who were of the time. I had a hundred paperbacks like his. We absorbed his airy-fairy gobbledygook through open pores, thrilled we had ears to hear what a sold-out world beyond campus was deaf to. At the teach-in, a lanky kid, greasy mop and scraggly facial hair, who'd been on the road, "California to the New York Island," and spoke with a Woody Guthrie beat shared his epiphany: "Everywhere I met kids puffing weed, popping pills, the greening of America, the new world coming. We'd never met before, but knew each other better than our families." A newborn child of the Sixties, I knew what he meant.

Then, in transcendental stratosphere, I became a genuine flower child for ten hours, "coming down" to discover I'd been drugged. It was the '73 graduation reception for parents relieved to retrieve peacenik offspring from the likes of me, sipping punch with awkward relatives. Returning home in an exalted state I took a hot shower to come back to earth, only to fire my rapture, pelting what muddled mind I had left into a nether world of old mythologies. At some point Carol woke in a panic to discover I'd been showering two hours. I began losing reality, got really lost, saw a streetlight out the window, one real thing. Until dawn I kept focus on the street light . . . the street light.

After the graduation ceremony I snagged George Greer, a just-minted grad, for a final chat. He was one of Pat's disciples later to do experimental psychiatry with therapeutic hallucinogens. I told him I nearly reached Nirvana, yet got lost in terror. George said I was drugged. Really. One of his friends spiked a cup with Mescaline meant for an old fogey he despised, but I got it.

Those were "the best of times, the worst of times." Best was education innovation, democratized Democracy, a shock-wave to ossified values, doors flung wide to healthier sexuality and gender-expanding disinhibition, end to draft and War. Students were the most alive and committed—by far—of any since I was young. All these events were occurring for the first time in my young life. If I later had a good idea, the seed was buried in that upheaval.

For many it was the worst of times: Cambodia and Kent State, SDS and Watergate, dirty hair and facial hair, "Nazi!" and "Fascist!" hurled at clueless senior citizens, tie-dyed hippies, unhygienic and discourteous, wailing "Puff the Magic Dragon" in bus stations, imperiously posturing bottom feeders of the rich, a great nation tuned in on itself.

How it became a movement, how I, not a student or under thirty, got in and got keeled over by it, is worth telling. First was the towering idealism of Dr. King's nonviolent outcry against War. The Sixties began with his Movement's freewheeling culture critique, miracle of solidarity and headwind of change. The Sixties began, in fact, with his death. Students went out from Columbia's memorial service to shut down the University. Malcolm X's bitter attack struck a chord with white radicals. It also awakened Stokely Carmichael's provocative phrase "black power," which inspired Mark Rudd's "student power" at Columbia's Students for a Democratic Society. SDS began with Tom Hayden's Port Huron Statement in 1960, which I didn't read until grad school. Hayden was my age and social class, but a Yankee. He admired the Movement, but being ignorant of Jim Crow cruelty, he was unimpressed by black radicalism. What drew him was black solidarity, their focused, indignant rage, their joyous community.

What racism did for the Movement, Vietnam did for the Students. Males were to be drafted, invading their privileged lives. They began "days of rage" and set loose a new social movement. Nixon invaded Cambodia, and Students became incendiary. At Kent State, compliant middle-American students demonstrated, an ROTC building caught fire, the governor, hurling inflammatory insults, activated the National Guard who fired bullets. Nine students were wounded as on a battlefield, four dead, America at war against its youth. Kids, only yesterday deferential to authority, poured out of dorms and Greek houses leaving books still opened on study tables. On that single day, passions and mutinous instincts of human solidarity were set loose. The next, colleges across the nation shut down. For a rapturous, transcendental moment, American Studenthood was a commune.

Beginning in 1959, Ken Kesey's psychedelic antics inspired Students' most radical break with Establishment. Ginsberg, Leary, Wolft, The Grateful Dead turned celebrative psychedelics into a religion of the young. Social movements are spiritual, characterized by mystical unity and elevated common mind, aided in this case by hallucinogens.

And the pill was first approved as contraceptive in 1960, same year as the sit-ins and Port Huron Statement. Adolescent girls, "on the pill" by college, were not about to be locked in "women's dorms" protected in "parietal hours" from horny men by colleges "*in loco parentis.*" Before demonstrating against war, they marched against parietal hours. A popular anti-Vietnam placard was "MAKE LOVE, NOT WAR." The enemy had been the near-inevitability of pregnancy. Betty Friedan's '59 *The Feminine Mystique* shattered the image of pregnancy-dominated females. Girls on the pill became Women! —out to change themselves and the world, politically seizing their own education.

The '69 Stonewall riots, the "New Sexuality," and the Students' wholesale rejection of old values, made Gay and Lesbian coming out something imminently to do. Straight men faced the draft. Gay Men just came out—and got a medical deferment!—a joyous subversion of the system against itself. In the Movement, students were gay and straight together.

The Sixties' signature was its music, elevating the common soul, propagating its themes: Amazing Grace; Woody Guthrie's old movement songs; Pete Seeger's "We Shall Overcome;" Dylan; Guthrie; Baez; Collins; Peter, Paul & Mary; Hair. These were in the air and airwaves, tuneful music, inspiring lyrics (Dylan's being the best poetry of the generation), all fun and beautiful, uplifting and communal, music to dance to. The Grateful Dead made it a cult. The '69 Woodstock Festival, as the '63 March on Washington for the Movement, drew together outdoors the entire Sixties spectrum: pot, hallucinogens, free love, long hair, peace signs, naked gay men, liberated women, and music, the pantheon of great ones blaring, pulsing, soaring across the countryside.

Exempt from the draft and sexual revolution, I had no characteristics of the decade. I was a Baptist preacher! I thought marijuana fun (it made me giggle) but hated the smoke. I'd barely heard of Vassar until forty hours before arriving. I was finished as a student when I joined the Student Movement. I was faculty for god's sake, "over thirty," disqualified. What happened? I was set up. I visited Vassar a week before Kent State, ten months after Stonewall, eight after Woodstock, just before "Amazing Grace" hit the charts. Four months later I was there: thirty-five miles from Woodstock, twenty from Timothy Leary's estate, eighty miles upriver from the heart of feminism and the Stonewall Bar, fifteen from Pete Seeger's house, the veritable eye of this storm. Within a week I was leading the movement in "Amazing Grace." My other instances of being jerked around were traumatic. This one, Baptist preacher to Sixties chaplain, sheer ecstasy. There was evidence of the Demonic in the sixties. Yet I never saw a building burn, a billy-club or mace attack. In our communal womb I heard the Establishment's rage, but distantly. Up close it was more or less beautiful.

These kids seemed to have read as much as I had and were more articulate in issues of the moment, in nuanced opposing camps ("Are you Maoist, Trotskyist or pure Leninist?" "Pacifist, or ready to commit violence?"), the epitome of engaged. Despite my newly-minted academic pedigree I needed catching up. I was intimidated but thrilled by a generation who took issues I'd been academic with as the stuff of life, worthy of risk. I didn't know what they knew, but I wanted to, and they were willing to take me. It was lonely and humiliating to be white in The Civil Rights

Movement, but here were middle-class whites inspired by the Movement like me. I wasn't a student, but I was closer to them than I was to the angry, somber black marchers going to jail. I was in love with the students because they were in love with Martin Luther King, and yet were non-black. It was sheer Grace to be drafted into their wake.

Homophobia

The Stonewall Bar in Greenwich Village, where drag queens were arrested after considerable resistance, referred to simply as "Stonewall," generally regarded as the beginning of the US Gay Rights Movement, is eighty miles from Vassar. I was unaware of Stonewall when I became pastor to the movement's future national leaders twelve months later. One week in I learned the term "Come out," entertained my first thought about homosexuality, and met my first affirmative gay person and first lesbian. My flock, some terrified at themselves and their new notoriety, were looking to my chaplaincy for leadership.

A Florida orange juice queen, movie star and sister Southern Baptist made headlines quoting biblical condemnations of them. They asked me for comment. I put them off, leafed through scripture getting no guidance, jotted down some contrary thoughts (a trial run) and put them out. A week later I woke to find my jottings as an Op Ed column in the *New York Times*, soon reprinted in a dozen papers. I got religious homophobic hate mail, but also invitations—specifically as a Baptist preacher—to speak to the morality of a movement I only barely knew existed. Reeling from exposure as a sexist pig, I was suddenly a public spokesman for whatever the LGBTQ Movement was. And this before I discovered I was homophobic. I'd been capsized again. Whiplash!

I looked up "homophobic" in my pocket dictionary. No such word. It wasn't in my *Scrabble Dictionary* either. In the Gothic cathedral-like Vassar library, in the unabridged dictionary opened on what looks like a pulpit, no "homophobic." I fished for a definition of the no-such-word without actually revealing I didn't know. "Fear of homosexuals," a gasping, tear-splotched counselee blurted, who'd just told me she was afraid of herself. At first I thought that an oxymoron. Who could be afraid of these gentle, awkward, uncertain children? Then, suddenly I realized I was.

What in dictionaries didn't exist, existed, I discovered with horror, in myself. I noted it first with Meg, a petite, fresh-faced freshman who came out in counseling. She described a background of church, family warmth, secure friendships and emotional health, but upon entering the sexually diverse environment of Vassar she'd awakened a deeper reality. "I'm lesbian." She wanted advice, what to do. The chill that shot down my spine rebounded in a chilling mental image: Meg in a dark, smoky subterranean space—as in our maid Nancy's basement space—being pawed and leered at by husky, mannish females suggesting lewd, disgusting unimaginable erotic involvements. Where did that come from? I'd had enough clinical training to know something inappropriate to the counseling relationship was going on, and to avoid imposing it on Meg. I have no idea what I said.

The next afternoon, Barry, a skinny, pimply-faced sophomore, came out too. This time the chill came up from the solar plexus, a defensive reaction, lest Barry, having come out, should come on to me. Whatever I said or didn't say to Barry (clearly not the jolt of irrational dread I was feeling – doubtless something innocuous that was taken to be tolerant and liberal) got out, resulting in an invitation to speak to "Gayvassar," an unregistered, underground network. Should I go? What would I say? What would straight people think? That I was gay? Would they be right?

"Homophobia," the irrational terror of homosexual culture, of confrontation with homosexual people, the dread otherness of homosexual reality, and especially of the same-sex affections rumbling within one's own self, implies a psychological—phobic—complex. But my scant acquaintance with the literature of primitive religion (Joseph Campbell, Mircea Eliade, Rudolph Otto, etc.) informed my self-diagnosis with symbols sunk far beneath the reach of psychology. I think of the Latin phrase, *mysterium tremendum et fascinans*. You don't have to know its literal meaning to feel its dread radiance. Though penned by Otto, a conservative religionist, the phrase has nonetheless shaped me. This was much more serious, multidimensional and fateful than a mere phobia, the measly psychological. The word "Satanic" came to mind.

I was in the grip of possession, a macabre terror of layered malignant threats regarding association with this thing. The surface threat was from my familiar society, the risk of an alienation far worse than mine from Dixie, of ruin. Beyond that was the ghastly image of a hauntingly dark culture beneath my own. There was the threat of demonic challenges coming up from down there, for me to side with, embrace, sink into. But beneath it all, most horrific of all, was profound ontological uncertainty: What if I was one? What if reality itself was on the verge of inversion?

In truth, I'm far too repressed to have allowed anything like the drama of this dread to crawl up to consciousness. What I did know is that what I'd stumbled into, this "homophobia," is a morass of universal Evil in which we are truly all together, and from which we will not be released—except together.

Anti-Semitism and Hitler

Another thing I didn't know was that Vassar was forty percent Jewish and half were from Catholic backgrounds. A few were vaguely Protestant, but the majority, whatever the background, were born-again secular. I seemingly alone was Southern Baptist, but pastor and religion teacher (rabbi?) to a thousand Jews; most, I'd learn, were in dire need of help with their religion. This was exploded out of proportion when, just as secular elitists were absorbing the shock of a Southern Baptist chaplain, the president of the Southern Baptist convention made banner headlines with a statement of unprecedented antisemitism: "God does not hear the prayer of a righteous Jew."

Was it true? I hadn't thought about it since Second-Ponce de Leon. But upon reading the *New York Times* headline on my doorstep, I had a short walk to religion class to decide. Leading faculty were Jewish, most polemically secular, many offended by a chaplaincy in a secular college, let alone a Southern Baptist. And twenty Jewish students were eager for my views at the end of my walk. With the headline cycling my brain, an unacknowledged cesspool erupted in my soul. It was an encyclopedia of demonic meaning I wouldn't deconstruct for another two decades, when, in a fit of horrified discovery, I would track down and read every word. Triggered by the headline, I was sunk in memories of Ike Blumberg's defiled house.

In few events has the fatal flaw, the wicked potential of humanity, been so manifest as in the Holocaust. What I knew about it and the Nazis was little advanced beyond newsreels, mounds of frail, bald and naked corpses, near-corpses sheared and slope shouldered in ragged rows, revelations about gas chambers and furnaces. Death camp survivors seemed hardly human, and represented just short of a hundred percent of Jews I'd ever knowingly seen. I'd heard Daddy, in his signature disgust, identify Hollywood rascals as "Jews," and Kitty warn about Ike's house.

Buried in my inner silence, from the Vast Unspoken regarding the Holocaust, was the unacknowledged implication that "the Jews" had somehow deserved it. What the damning headline and the turbulence of soul I suffered as I walked to class that day had to do with the Holocaust I wouldn't get for years. As for what I said in class—I have no idea.

An ironic footnote: The day after the anti-Semitic quote from the Southern Baptist president, the Times ran an op-ed rebuttal to his anti-Semitism, by William Keucher, president of the American Baptist Convention. Twenty years later I would be an American Baptist and amazingly, Dr. Keucher's pastor. And he would once again be making headlines. But that time his attack would be against American, not Southern Baptists, who would come out as officially homophobic. Who he'd be defending would be me.

Along the way I took up the study of Nazism. Whatever Nazis were, they were religious. Being a sensationalist kind of guy, I used a Nazi propaganda film produced the year before my birth for "Intro Religion," my best device for depicting the religious as a dimension of life. The Nazis were a social movement—a reality I'd missed, assuming social movements inherently redemptive. The film (banned in the US until Germany was defeated and their charismatic leader dead) showed Nazism to be the most religious modern revitalization movement. Nazi's antecedents were traditions from ancient India brought to the Rhine Valley by Aryan migrations, and the thunderous mythic complex of Rhine River tribal gods with which Aryans synchronized.

More important to Nazism was Martin Luther, charismatic leader of the German Reformation, "the greatest anti-Semite," said a prominent Nazi, "who ever lived." His translation of the Bible is called the genesis of modern German, made earthy and rich by its resonance with Germanic myths. Luther also infused Jewish biblical rhetoric with, ironically, his vitriolic hatred of Jews. His Bible and the unrestrained violence of his oratory against Jews, Anabaptists and Catholics is thoroughly Germanic in its transcendental brutality.

Several Nazi leaders came from the *Thule Gesellschaft,* a religious cult with explicit links to violent, anti-Semitic, Aryan-supremacist traditions. Hitler's oratorical coach was charismatic leader of the *Thule Gesellschaft,* Dietrich Eckhart, who taught him to thunder these symbols like a screaming evangelical preacher, giving him hypnotic rhythms, mythic themes and subliminal images to evoke ecstatic response from followers. All my life I've known Baptist preachers who expertly do this with the Bible. Richard Wagner was Hitler's spiritual father. His *Ring des Niebelungen* transformed German spirituality into a gloriously violent culture-religion. Wagner's charismatic Siegfried inspired Hitler. Wagner's was the music of the movement—his "Amazing Grace."

Under Hitler's anti-Jewish, anti-Catholic, pagan dictatorship, mainstream German Christianity was sucked into the Nazi religiousness. The German Church came into a demonic synchronization with religious Nazism, much like the melding of Jim Crow and Southern Baptist spirituality. It called itself "Positive Christianity," an ecstatic, transcendental "Yes!" to the religious enthusiasm being generated, swastika banners alongside crosses in sanctuaries; swastika insignia and holstered lugers worn to church, Nazi implications in mind singing, "Ein Feste Burg ist unser Gott" (A mighty fortress is our God—Luther's Reformation hymn). I was reminded of the Stars and Bars unfurled, during my youth, in Southern churchyards, and the religious fervor singing "Dixie".

Hitler's oratory, as with Baptist preachers and charismatics in most religions, was not meant to be rational discourse. It was singsong calling out of symbols, mythic themes, appeals to tribal loyalties and transcendental hungers, tones resonant with ritual currents, rhythms generative of chanted liturgical response. It intended not to enlighten or persuade, rather to convert, subject, enflame. His was not a theistic religion, despite occasional Machiavellian references to "God." It is animistic, a cataclysmic drama eternally underway in "blood" and "soil." Nazis greeted him and each other with raised arm and open palm, a gesture from religious rituals (evangelical Protestantism for instance) signifying infusion of Spirit, as through a lightning rod, and the greeting "Heil Hitler!"— "Heil" suggestive of "heilig," holy. Hitler led mass torch-lit marches emblazoned with gigantic red swastika-emblazoned banners and the bent cross of Aryan religion. These are classic processions into ritual time and the "Cathedral of Light," sacred space.

The Cathedral of Light greatly dwarfed the great Catholic cathedrals of Europe. It was constructed by one hundred fifty anti-aircraft searchlights borrowed from spotting enemy bombers over cities, transported to Nuremburg to create a spectacular cone of beams touching the clouds, one of the grandest religious artifacts ever conceived, the ultimate setting for Hitler's charisma. I recognized it instantly, having been so deeply moved in the constructed sacred spaces of mass Billy Graham Crusades.

The Nazi film I used was *Triumph of the Will* by Leni Riefenstahl, often called the greatest of all documentaries. It is propagandistic presentation of the Nuremburg Festival celebrating Hitler's ascension to power. The film opens to marching military formations, not with guns, but brooms and pitchforks—a defeated, disarmed people heroically rising up. Then comes Hitler in an open-cockpit airplane making messianic descent through the clouds. A torch lit parade makes grand entrance into the Cathedral of Light. Hitler, suggestive of my first thrilling sight of Billy Graham, mounts the podium between towering swastika banners, bellowing in fulsome *Thule-Gesellschaft* oratory. His black-booted feet are like trunks, rooted in the "soil," his frame swaying, gesturing wildly, a rooted oak in the winds of History. Hitler was Siegfried on the stage at Bayreuth, his voice in rhythmic cadences of Lutheran German, images of river cults, the Brothers Grimm, Wagner, calling the totemistic Aryan tribe to rise miraculous from eclipse to a destined glory, evoking atavistic passion... religious pageantry at its most extravagant. It is profoundly Evil, like nothing modern, like religious passions of the old biblical warlords.

VASSAR STORIES

Vassar Chapel, where I writhed through an enthused decade with its children, is a huge, seductively gorgeous architectural nightmare, toward the dark end of a spectrum from Gothic to Baroque, evocative of days when the demonic was at hand. It crouches behind thick stone walls as of a fortress, behind heavy leaded doors whose closings evoke the word "slammer."

Its cavernous interior, whose massive volume swallowed the modest congregations my quirky preaching drew, is arched by two dozen beams above a hundred ribs of brown pews below, barely lighted by Tiffany windows' darkly arty colors. Getting to the bathroom required stumbling from my office across a darkened balcony high above ribs of dark, descending a gloomy vortex to the basement, down a long dark hallway to nowhere.

The Chapel Board (my commune of subversive co-conspirators) christened it "Freudian Cathedral" because of its haunting aspect, and because, like all things Freudian, it's determined by its organ, its proudest and most prominent part. Phallic pipes, as students inexpertly fingered its several manuals, squealed and thundered through the day distracting whatever went on there. It got "tuned," an agonizing two day ordeal when rank upon rank of pipes were tormented into pitch like wailing cats. Its metabolism of schedules dominated the life and services of the building like adolescent testosterone. And when rightly handled, as it regularly was, it exploded in aesthetic ecstasy.

The Chaplain's Office, where for eleven years I did my thing, is a spacious, beamed room lit by arched, leaded, gothic windows, book-lined in mahogany shelves, furnished in antiques from alumnae. Its studded floor was covered by a probably priceless Persian carpet, freshly cleaned when I first arrived. The office sits high atop a twisting stone staircase, half up the phallic, campus-dominating steeple. It was there I learned exorcism.

The Chapel Board met there, and among other things planned

Sunday services. Most were conventional enough, with gorgeous renditions by the organ and college choir, but the movement kids had something to work out—and, I suppose, I did—and needed ritual space. Lots of people not of the moment, not with the process, were frightened and run off.

The organist was horrified. The college president said during my interview, with fervent Oxbridge reserve, that he considered himself "a veritable pillar of the chapel," but he and his wife quit coming not long into my tenure. Who got it and went with the flow was Jim Marvin, flamboyant choir director. Sundays I'd push open the heavy medieval door to be knocked nearly down by magnificent sounds from the choir loft, Jim shouting encouragement above angel harmonies. Jim was fired before I was, the charge being "not intellectual enough," but really for being one of us. Happily, he was snatched by the Harvard Glee Club for thirty-odd years of choir-shouting and great distinction.

We took January retreats on the snowy summit of Storm King Mountain overlooking, ironically, the US Military Academy at West Point. Actually we were at the base, the summit accessed by a narrow path, winding uncertainly up a cliff facing the Hudson River. Successive Januaries the fragile path was covered impassably by an ice slick. Somehow, half a hundred of us would make it up nonetheless, none tumbling off to death as we surely should have.

Every spring I'd gather eager faculty geniuses for what we called "Ethical Issue Courses." These were outside departments, unfunded and multidisciplinary. We'd do a current issue (Apartheid, Nuclear Disarmament, Feminism) then notify faculty, "If you in your expertise have something to say, join us." Lots did. Most had never taught or researched from overtly ethical perspective and came with excitement. Each, from different disciplines, would give one lecture, advocating away by means of what they knew, spewing indignation like Amos the Prophet, of whom they'd never heard, indignant at the injustice in question, plotting partisan strategies for reform. We offered the lectures to the public. The faculty conversations, let alone the classes, were turbulent, demons of public injustice working out through intellectual struggles of incredibly bright people. One outcome was a sprouting, like mushrooms in the college catalogue of regular courses in "Apartheid," "Nuclear Disarmament," etc.

On the day of the seasonal time change I headed home on my bike to discover it was pitch dark. The chaplain's residence ("Ferrell House" after a donor of that name) was at the far end of a lakeside path. Mounting my old rust of a bike, I proceeded confidently, as in everything, as if I could see where I headed, into the lake. When I slogged drenched, mud-caked and glasses-less into the supper-lit kitchen, Carol said, "I didn't know it was raining." It wasn't. It was me, falling again, doing what I do, another parable of the times. Peter, Dan and Chris were bribed with quarters to go in the icy waters for my glasses.

I was on that path twice a day for eleven years, a favorite place. One spring I ambled it with a student. He plucked a young leaf from a vine and ate it. It was poison ivy. He said he ate it every spring for a week when it budded, for immunity. I yielded to his encouragement, had one myself, and for a month sported an anal itch. I mentioned this to a biologist friend who assured me that I could have had the reaction in my throat and choked to death. True to the times, however, despite the unfortunate itch, I never suffered poison ivy rash again.

This path was magical landscape, as picturesque and complex in its ecology as were the Seventies. There hangs on my wall a haunting scene from it, a stark, black and white wintertime tangle of bare limbs, a splotch of deciduous green slightly off center. I'd watched the artist, our local Picasso, Louis Rubenstein, painting it and other path scenes on many a bike ride home. It was given to me by my Vassar friends as my departure gift—after I was fired.

Ralph, a wispy-haired senior with long skinny legs, and Gini, brunette, considerably less skinny, asked for a wedding. His selective service number was up. Both hated war, but didn't want to flee to Canada as some did. So Ralph stretched his skinny leg on a Chapel step and Gini, sobbing, jumped onto it, smashed it at the knee joint causing more or less permanent damage, exorcising the demon of war, opening for their friends, whose colorful signatures splattered the cast he drug down the aisle, an heroic future.

Hardly a week passed when someone didn't come in to come out, to process whether to forsake the demonic closet's privileged, counterfeit life and plunge into the maelstrom of gay reality—still a most fateful decision. Or a recent ex-virgin woman frantic over which tragedy to embrace: the shameful ordeal of abortion or the unsupportable new life in her womb; an unwanted, potentially disastrous future, or a profoundly disillusioned sexual future. I found myself presiding over too many divorces in those sexually charged days. A colleague and his exceptional wife, our close friends, had joined in the epidemic sexual insanity and, wholly unsuited for each other, come to the inevitable parting. He came in sobbing. They'd made love and cried all night, packed her car and she'd driven away.

Another couple, both of mythical sexual beauty, lived the idyllic perfect marriage, their paradise being each other, but were unable to speak what wasn't perfect or even that there was ever a problem. They'd imploded and had affairs, seeking paradise again. By the time they got to me, the demon was the irresistibly seductive but ruined carcass of their marriage. I'd help them separate, but they'd be drawn like magnets back to each other's beds for more ecstatic torment. I didn't help much, but they found new loved ones. Two lesbians for whom I'd done a secret wedding were drawn down exciting but tragically incompatible paths. A Catholic priest friend, in love with one of my students, moved in with her.

One wedding was of a man with seven children from an earlier marriage, and a young woman. The wedding involved the kids, so the congregation included their squirming friends. The ritual, of the times, was far from conventional. As my daughter's friend, Emily, skipped out, I asked what she thought. "You didn't do it right," she announced. "What was wrong?" I asked, defensive, disappointed.

"You didn't say . . ." she struggled for the omitted traditional words, "'Do you take this man . . .'" she said, still struggling—then, got it—"to be your awful wedded wife." The times.

Mike McCarthy philosopher, deeply committed Catholic, beloved friend, is Emily's father. We used to regularly have it out, the philosopher defending religion, the religionist, professional holy man, attacking. On our last day before my exile, we did battle on a walk through the Vassar woods. Emerging back onto a manicured landscape, we looked at each other and broke into hysterics. Mike always appears just off the pages of *GQ* and was, as usual, immaculate. I, who'd stepped exactly where he had, was covered in brambles.

At the last Chapel Board meeting, we did a ritual vacuuming of my carpet, last cleaned when I moved in. By then it held detritus from several thousand confessions of eleven years. To "Amazing Grace" we solemnly vacuumed it, poured blackened grains into an emptied Gallo bottle from after-Chapel Sherry Hours (I'd used it as a water decanter for the decade), stuck a candle in its neck, burned it down to a cap of dribbled wax. My icon from the Seventies.

Cliff got through college in ROTC. When he enlisted he had a PhD and got a faculty position at West Point. He and I mostly lost touch in intervening years, but when I went to Vassar, he did Army Reserve time there, just down the Hudson. Our reunion, howling reconstructions of Buckhead Sundays, was near the time of the "Amazing Grace" episode. It was then that "Grace" began to dawn as the name of our adventures. By then, twice upended, I began thinking through those stories, with Cliff, as moments of Grace. Next summer, when I trekked down to watch "Major Hendrix, Sir" snappily saluted by plebes and to make fun of him, I'd been jerked around thrice more. In the late night, alcohol-laced Me-and-Cliff retellings of those traumas, I learned to call them all Grace, and to reconstitute my life.

The ending of my eleven years at Vassar (what a great job!) had ambiguous consequences. Students were the prophetic minority then, open to anything, up for moral risk. I had platform to teach courses, conduct worship, lead forums, retreats, demonstrations, hang out my counseling shingle, address public controversies from overt moral concern, and nourish students' prophetic persona. I regularly offended superiors with choices I believed right, and eventually lost my job: an anticipated, willingly accepted consequence. Truth is, when I left, I was ready to leave. Given my pastoral and activist commitments, I was never going to make the front ranks of academic scholarship. My gifts, such as they were, were more suited for church—if I could find one to put up with me. Furthermore, the circumstances of my separation from Vassar made me a cause célèbre, and that year the issues, essentially the moral-engagement side of academia, made it to the level of a social movement, me less at the head, more at the center.

I did a lot of grieving, being forcibly separated from that singularly great job. It was also extraordinarily exciting, and happily for me I landed on my feet in what was to be an even greater job. I was not literally fired. The powers, rather, gutted the office. Because of my choices, that college will never again empower anyone to do such things as it enabled me to do. This, after a long line of great predecessors, is my legacy.

Thinking from Down Under

I began to think at Vassar. Having been knocked over multiple times, I thought from the underside of everything I'd been. The context was my role as teacher to the signature Students of the century, that mass movement of adolescents who for a decade wielded the moniker "Student" in deep anger and great joy.

"The things which I had seen" (Wordsworth) from church and the Buckhead woods, "I now could see no more," an existential concern I took out on three generations of Vassar kids. It was a course—for myself. Not "Disenchantment" (who would sign up for Disenchantment?), but "Secularization," a respectable concept. Students were secular, but knew most of humanity had been religious. I lured them to see what had happened to them.

We examined secularized religion. The Reformation defaced Catholic beauty and mystery, Dietrich Bonhoeffer carrying worldly Protestantism to its inevitable conclusion, "religion-less Christianity," "Christ of the marketplace," upended religion as I inhabited it. We traced urbanization, industrialization and destabilization. These had uprooted simple souls from sacred soil, lifelong community, holy rites handed down, mythic memories continuous with centuries, simple, immediate beliefs—and that for anonymous towns where no god ever walked, jobs no father ever worked, toiling too many hours for too little pay and no satisfaction. Gas chambers, crematoriums. And colonialism. European domination of the "primitive" world, discrediting local traditions, with secular culture and secularized Protestantism, controlled eighty-five percent of the earth. As a post-reconstruction southerner, I'd grown up colonized. Finally, revolution: the Marxists criminalizing religion as fabricated by unjust economics—the most secularizing event of all. By now I was dabbling in Marx.

"God is dead, and we have killed him." Thus spake Zarathustra, Nietzsche's lyrical secular mystic, meaning the West's triumphal overthrow of religion and conventional morality, both of which were regressive. I found Nietzsche more exciting than anything else I was reading or had yet read.

This was the "why" and "how" of secularization. As for "what happened?" we read *The Teachings of Don Juan*, a fictional story of an anthropologist studying a Native American shaman who claimed to "see," in peyote rituals, spirits appearing and disappearing and bodily flights over the landscape. Don Juan, humorously noting the scientific detachment and skepticism of the young scientist, shocked him by declaring him "called" to be a shaman himself. With intensifying ambiguity, students watched "one of us" betray scientific commitments, and in a harrowing denouement, go over to "the other side," the unmodern world, releasing grip on modern consciousness and recovering what was lost.

Sensitive students asked, "What was lost?" Did medieval artists "really see" the angels and demons in their paintings? Did they know something we don't, that lives danced morning to night, into seasons, years and life stages with ritual? They were cloaked by mystery, landscaped by sacred symbols, overseen by awesome gods, bounded by taboos, invested with meanings handed down, pointing every moment beyond this mere world. What mysteries, no longer apparent, did they entertain? What magic, no longer credited, did they practice? What demons did they exorcize? I had no idea—yet another failure.

I knew what I had lost: laughing at the Bible with Cliff, giving up not-dancing-for-God, college learning in forbidden knowledge. I knew what I had been and was no more, and what the quotient of loss was, subtracting one from the other. But not, beyond enchantment and religion as the core of common life, what we had lost, the modern West as a matter of civilization. I didn't know what I was born having lost. Suddenly, I needed to know.

So I hauled Peter (six), Dan (five), Chris (two) and Carol to London, and holed up in the British Museum. We got a Hampstead flat and a barely functioning English Ford for excursions. One was with a friend from York, a Romantic Poets scholar, to the Lake

District, seeking what Wordsworth "now could see no more." I worked in the Museum's book-lined Reading Room where Marx worked. I chose the four great secularizers of the intellectual West: Machiavelli, Galileo, Marx and Darwin. But not themselves. Rather, the unmodern people's reaction. What was there before, and what was lost thereafter.

I began with reaction to the first modern book, at first an unbearable insult, then an honored breakthrough. Hardly a book, more a memorandum (eighty handwritten pages), it began as *De Principalitatibus* (*Of Principalities*) and ended *Il Principe* (*The Prince*), the author, Niccolo Machiavelli, a sixteenth century Florentine diplomat, finding no savior for his principality but a starkly drawn political individual. He wrote it in six months, on the side, among much else a major landmark in the literary landscape of my life.

The Prince (elegant, rational, value-free) hypothesizes how politics works, arrives with empirical observation at conclusion and, fatefully, confirmed by subsequent history. Science! A breakthrough! He "proved," stated starkly with unprecedented dispassion, that religious princes failed. Successful ones, cunning, deceitful and ruthless, "simulate" but don't believe religion. He wrote this as if it were okay. In *The Prince*'s pages, religion (contrasted with the "appearance of religion") disappears. Also morality, true speech and every sacred value, three centuries before there was a philosophy to span the vacuum. What appears is the autonomous human mind and a host of demonic practices, camouflaged by the "pretext of religion," in other words, everything modern to dread: insubstantial religion, phony religious behavior, religion with the virtue gone out of it being its hallmark. For the people, something dreadful happened because of *The Prince*. Whoever can read its maxims without their horror have, for good or ill, succumbed to what they feared. I have, as had my students.

I turned to Galileo. According to his telescope, contradicting Bible and common experience, the earth (not the center of the universe) moves, is not sequestered directly beneath the watchful eye of God, is not what the Bible says it is.

I plunged into the Museum's thousands of anti-Darwin publications, giving eloquent voice to the horror at his desecration of the Creation stories. According to Darwin, no god knelt, scooped soil with Divine hands, shaped a human form, breathed into its nostrils the breath of life, or gave it meaning and purpose. There was, rather, a brutal, soulless process, "red in tooth and claw."

There were two heart-rending moments of loss in our London pilgrimage. At Trafalgar Square, Danny, who suffered a propensity for losing things, lost his Beefeater, a foot-high likeness of a palace guard. He loved the Beefeater, an astonishingly glorious souvenir and stretch for our budget. While we took pictures of pigeons on our heads, he laid it on a bench—and it was gone. His wailing grief inflated my swelling sense of loss. I still weep at the memory.

Chris left her blanket, companion in dreamland every night and nap time, on a Rhine River boat. Like Linus in Peanuts, she and her blanket were inseparable. Its silky fringe chewed, stiffened and nasty, the weave worn nearly through, it was her totem. Her shriek on missing it rent the night. Looking for lodging in nighttime Rhinish streets, we imagined Chris— and we—would never sleep again. Her sobbing was beyond unbearable. I settled them and went into the dark night of the soul on a fool's mission to rescue the blanket, and us all, driving fifty miles through the alien gloom to the boat's last stop. I found the docked boat, darkened. Unable to remember German for "blanket," I mounted the deck, and there it was, a lone, blanket-draped chair. Back in our room, Chris still gasping and heaving, her brothers tucked lovingly around her, took the blanket into her grief-swollen mouth and fell to sleep. I felt I'd found a lost talisman of childhood. Of course I hadn't. I was into Darwin, laughing at religion, reducing it to a worn-out, spittle-crusted rag of a blanket, in the home to Rhine River gods worshiped centuries before Moses—lost before Darwin.

Darwin was buried in Westminster Abbey. That year another Londoner, a German political economist and *New York Tribune* stringer, was buried in Highgate Cemetery, unmarked pauper's grave #15054. It was Karl Marx.

A wonderfully ironic story echoed in the British Museum Reading Room where Marx worked—and now, I did. An ancient librarian in the nineteen twenties was asked if he remembered Marx. He eyed the past. "Marx... Dr. Marx... Yes," his craggy face lifted. "Massive gray beard... came every day... over there... then ... was gone—and," shrugging frail shoulders, "never heard from again."

In Marx, oppressive, insubstantial religion, displaced by beneficent, material revolution, would evaporate. In those secular days, alienated from Baptist religion, I believed. Marx is a conjunction of profundity and naïveté. Naïve are his uninformed prejudices about religion, the alleged "inevitability" of evolutionary dialectic, a supposedly transient destiny for state, proletarian dictatorship, class conflict, romanticism about the proletariat. But he was an earthquake of mind. His critiques of bourgeois life, democracy and capitalism sparkle with original insight and articulate the masses' experience, and to a degree, mine. His critique of religion, as more religiously sophisticated friends Engels and Kautsky point out, echoes Hebrew Prophets and Jesus. I found unanswerable, also, "The beginning of all criticism ... is the criticism of religion," epithets which became shibboleths for liberal intellectuals. And revolutionary Marxist states outlawed religion. It really was disappearing.

On a memorable day I took my *Marx and Engels on Religion* paperback to Highgate Cemetery. It was raining, ubiquitous London. Among a forest of teetering crosses and crumbling angels was the bearded bust erected by later Marxists—grave #15054.

Chiseled on it, from his theses on Feuerbach: "The philosophers have sought to explain the world. The point, however, is to change the world." Through a soggy day, occasionally glancing at the great bust and comic landscape of grimy crosses, aslant as though toppled by an earthquake radiating from it, soaked through but thrilled, I read his attack on religion. It was a piercing articulation of precisely my experience with Jim Crow religion. I still keep the old paperback, its pages curled and yellowed, a pilgrimage icon. *Marx and Engels on Religion*, along with *The Prince*, left me constitutionally incapable of taking anything religious at face value.

What was Lost

What I read in the British Museum was not these giants, but reaction to them. Terror and dread at Galileo's telescope lasted longest. Worst and angriest was rage at Machiavelli's alleged cynicism. I found over three hundred plays from the Machiavelli legend in Elizabethan drama, one hundred sixty diabolical characters. Their names give the flavor of the reaction: "Match-a-villian," "Hatch-a-villain," "Matchless Villain," "Mach-evill," "Hatch-evill," "That evil none can match," "Vile Machaville," "Instrument of Satan," "Devil turned moralist," "Incarnation of Judas." These weren't names for a lonely, faithful, Florentine Catholic, but something demonic inserted in the essence of the body politic.

Anti-Darwinism eclipsed both and survives yet in contemporary schools founded to not-teach evolution, which nonetheless teach Galilean science. The tragic-comic Scopes trial, which took place shortly after the founding of Protestant Fundamentalism, dramatizes what seemed at the time a last, futile rear-guard action against the evaporation of western religion.

I read Freud on religion as pathological "illusion." It seemed for and about me. I read Einstein, said to be the smartest man in the world, whose elegant $E=mc^2$ is proof that nothing is as it seems, but "relative" to matter, motion and time, inspiring outbreaks of philosophical relativism where absolutes—the basis of religion—all but disappear. And I read about the evangelical atheists, who declared religion and God frankly immoral. The sign that secularization was finally complete is that after five centuries of outcry, these last three hardly got a reaction. Ironically, about when I quit teaching Secularization, Reagan was elected, and secularization, not religion, began to "wither away."

Profound spirituality, of which I'm more or less incapable, comes with intense focused discipline, actually no less rarely in a secular age than ever. Unmodern spiritualism was more likely demonic than profound. What's been lost in secular modernity is rather a simple assumption of mystery, immediate awareness of miracle, instinctive dread of the Demonic, thrill at monumental presence. Lost is wonder, uncomplicated apprehension at miracle and magic. Lost are classic media to transcendence. We still have rationally constructed myth, symbol and ritual, and technological presentation of them in super-churches, which greatly exceeds what ancients could do. What's lost is myth, symbol and ritual as the simplest, most familiar phenomena in the world; immediate ability to inhabit a myth and wonder at it; dread of a symbol and trembling awe of it; delight in ritual, nourishing renewal drawn from it.

What the ancients interacted with, as described by anthropologists, really is lost. Of these interactions we have no tangible idea. Even if we did—if, on the borders of secular consciousness, miracle, mystery and transcendence seem occasionally to intrude—we can't grasp them. Or if we do, we can't assume our experience is shared, can't speak of them convincingly to others or find the proof our scientific mind requires that they are really there. Or use them... utility, the most universal contemporary value. We can't count or count on them. Like the nighttime dream on waking, they vanish with the dawn of thought. The loss was so protracted and gradual as to have been lost to memory, its inevitable grieving now seeming anachronistic. And for the body politic, as opposed to the rare spiritually disciplined individual, there's no way back.

There are still disciplined spiritualists, withdrawn from modernity, for whom such things aren't lost—perhaps as many as ever. I know and admire some. There are the sectarian Born-Again who, as William James observed from a secular perspective, are propelled beyond secularity by "true belief" and programmed indulgence in religious ecstasy. This, given soul-hunger on the one hand, and the religious enthusiasms of mass spectator sports and mass political movements, both revolutionary and reactionary, gives temporary relief from the arid flatness of secular un-spirituality. And of course, there is radical Islamic fundamentalism. But to me, and to the western masses in their daily existence, in the public realm itself, the very real world of Spirit is simply lost.

MARX AND JESUS

On the other hand, there was something familiarly religious in the true belief and passionate enthusiasms of scientists and Marxists, and even more in the radical spirit of the age. Student Movement rallies strongly resembled my childhood evangelical religion. Like other chaplains I found myself leading them. We were naturally drawn to these forms from professional expertise. This seemed coincidental, indeed comical. Movement kids were as likely anti-church as anti-war. Many were Jewish. Inspiration for rallies was the Civil Rights Movement, where connection with church was neither coincidental nor comical. The Montgomery Bus Boycott was a church event, led by preachers, nourished in Black Church Sanctuaries with pastoral care, prayer, Bible reading, hymn singing, preaching, infusions of Spirit—church people doing their religious thing. What they did in the streets started in church. Ironically, secular kids saw it in the streets, not in church, and liked it.

I stumbled on this while teaching "Radical Politics and Conscience." In Chapel Board and chapel I experimented with sacralization, joining the awakening spirit apparent among secular students. Using materials from my colleague, Pat Sullivan, I sought what was religious in social revolution. What Durkheim, Campbell and Eliade identify as "religious," despite their social conservatism, despite not noticing it themselves, is integral to social movements. I was experiencing it myself. Then I found it specifically spelled out in the anthropology of Anthony Wallace's concept of "Revitalization Movements."

Student rallies were spontaneous rituals, gathering and propelling a community in revolt beyond itself. Totemic insignia, like painted faces in ecstatic tribal sports gatherings, dissolved individual identity into mass manifestation of Being. Aging professors (this still marks academic peers in their eighth and ninth decades) felt naked without peace regalia, identifying to which tribe in the sacred order they belonged. We used music for communal affect, joining voice to elevate redemptive themes, old movement songs with implicit transcendental reference, spirituals from the Black Church such as "Amazing Grace," voices giving sweet expression to passionate commitments. Chants of "Peace Now!" and "Make Love, Not War!" were rhythmical call-and-response to an eternal imperative, as in gospel churches and tribal religions. We preachers preached on prophetic texts. As in Buckhead evangelism, we gave invitations to "Come forward," renounce the sinful, warring world, burn draft cards in ancient fiery sacrament, and join the redeemed Movement community.

There was generative role for myths and moral suasion, a tendency toward eschatology, charisma and revelation, making present what was never before imaginable. Processions, as in high church rituals, were passage into sacred time and space. Swaying bodily movements in sacred dance lifted gathered tribes together into universal life-flow, and ecstasy not uncommonly experienced was dissolution of self into the great beyond. All these were going on in social movements of the Seventies, often more than in religion. I used Movement films about Selma, the March on Washington, and Birmingham marches to illustrate primitive religion and religious phenomenology and provide introduction to what "the religious" is, not a particular "revealed" tradition, but a universal phenomenon.

But the religious is not religion. In this insight I start with Marx, based, like my interest, in revolutionary practice. He claimed the Jesus Movement was "Proto-communism," and might have been Communism sure enough had it not become a religion, an attractive insight but for the materialism. Marx's "really real" is material, economic, even religion, even the Jesus Movement. He didn't account for "Spirit," either of the Jesus or the Marxist Movement. Critiquing Jesus for becoming a religion, which I find convincing, he denies its "Spirit," which I don't. Marx said the Jesus Movement should have claimed its material base and created a materialist social structure. I evolved a different idea.

The Culinary Institute of America was just out my window at Yale. After I moved to Poughkeepsie, the "CIA" moved to an abandoned Jesuit monastery six miles from my house. I took Carol to a delicious student chef dinner. And there was Teilhard de Chardan's grave. At the CIA! A mid-twentieth century Jesuit in vogue with the Students, he died and was buried in the old monastery. Teilhard found God, or a vision of God, in Darwin! His pre-New Age theology, which I didn't like, included exactly what I'd been looking for. I read Asa Gray, Darwin's most enthusiastic American advocate, an evangelist of Darwinism, converting a generation of young Americans to his theory. His nineteenth century Darwinian movement reminded me of my students, though his students were being revitalized, not by social renovation but by "revelation of truth." So it was with Teilhard a generation later tapping the inspiration in Darwin's breakthrough. He put traditional religious imagery around it.

Einstein was not sophisticated in religion, yet through $E=mc^2$ he "saw" the "beauty," the "perfection" of the universe, and engaged Sacred reality through it. A demonic example is the Nazi Ernst Haeckel, who saw in Darwin the alleged evolutionary superiority of the Indo-Germanic race and grew ecstatic about it. His theory, borrowing from the nature-spirituality of German Romanticism, became a racist foundation for the Nazi movement.

My Secularization students were leading a Revitalization Movement, Sacralizing their culture. It was opening them to the Sacred, enchanting their disenchantment—the opposite of Secularization. That's what their social movement was, what I'd experienced in the movements that swept me up, a step toward my embrace of Grace. Something inspiring was going on. It had been going on among the scientists who'd helped cause secularization. Marx wasn't wrong about a material base. Upended, I'd landed on and embraced the worldly world, but Marx, in his enthusiasm for the base, ignored the thusi- (the Spirit) in his own en-thusi-asm.

It's with Marx that I name my condition "upended." He upended European thought, the world's social, political and economic reality. Specifically, he upended Hegel, his philosophical predecessor, and his fellow young Hegelian, Feuerbach. He "set Hegel," whose idealism, i.e., his dialectic of philosophical ideas, off his head, "on his feet;" i.e., on both the "really real," materialism, and the marching "feet" of revolutionary praxis. In my case, having lived by my Baptist spiritual ideas and my spiritual ascent toward an otherworldly Heaven, I was forcibly toppled from my religious head to my revolutionary feet by a series of powerfully material movements. Consequently, my successive ordeals of being upended included landing feet first in a stormy romance with Marxist materialism. I grew up with McCarthyism, the dread of communists. My conversion to Marx was not precipitous, like the others. It grew on me as a virtual creation of social movements. Having been driven, with newly minted academic skills, to research my disenchantment, I began to research social movements—the evolving subject of Radical Politics.

I lectured on Jack Reed's eyewitness account of the Bolshevik Revolution, *Ten Days that Shook the World.* Written in those days, it encapsulates the world-altering ferocity of an uprising people. A student, Susie Reed, wondered aloud if Reed might be "Uncle Jack," a skeleton in her conservative family closet. He was. She spent the semester studying this American journalist, the only non-Soviet buried in the Kremlin Wall (later played by Warren Beatty in the film "Reds") for broadcasting the revolution to the world. Suzie, a religion major with no job prospects, but gifted at squash, got on at *Saturday Review*'s squash team, then rode her genes to a distinguished journalistic career. She once did a *People* magazine cover story on her trip to Jack Reed institutions across Russia.

I was teaching in a multidisciplinary program on the "Freudo-Marxist Frankfurt School" whose ideas inspired students. For unknown reasons the program's anti-religious faculty included me, the chaplain. Maybe they thought me more radical, intellectual and "in" with Students than I was. Anyway, they took me, and fatefully paired me (courses boasted profs from different disciplines) with economist Eugen Loebl. About that time I hosted

David Halberstam, whose Pulitzer Vietnam articles were iconic among Students. Entering his faculty reception, he froze. "Loebl!" he barked, staring at Loebl across the room. "A great man! I covered his trial." I introduced them, mouth agape, arms akimbo, as one of the great journalists of our time ogled my new colleague. Eugen and the Students idolized each other. He'd been swept into the Czech Communist Movement, later rising to the Cabinet. With Moscow Bolsheviks, he fought Stalin's betrayal of the movement, was tortured and given a life sentence. Dubcek later released him, but when Dubcek's "Communism with a human face" was purged, Loebl fled west and to Vassar.

With Eugen, I entered the orbit of the Bolsheviks, modernity's most sweeping social movement. "Workers of the world unite; you have nothing to lose but your chains," penned by Marx at my British Museum table, transmuted into legend by Uncle Jack, borne to me by Loebl, silenced a decadent religion. But it also inspired, like newborn religions, a century's transforming passions. Revolutionary Marxism generated myths, symbols and rituals. It redeemed individual lives and common lives, stirred uprisings on every continent, reshaped the liberal worldview and redirected History. Inspiration happened in those ten days that shook the world. With Loebl and Uncle Jack, I got a taste.

Marx didn't pursue his insight, that the Jesus Movement was the first communist uprising short-circuited by religion, but Friedrich Engels, his collaborator and friend, did. Karl Kautsky made a career of it, finding a second precursor to modern Communism in sixteenth-century Anabaptists, my spiritual ancestors. Kautsky aimed to crush any flicker of Spirit from communist revolutions. He didn't succeed. Religion in the former Soviet Union is growing faster than anywhere except postcolonial Africa. This is a regressive development, perhaps, but denying the existence of Spirit, outlawing religion, is no more a remedy than "abstinence only" birth control.

My friend Bob Fortna and I taught "Marxism and the Book of Revelation." Bob, a New Testament scholar, taught Revelation—

the Bible's kookiest, most violent book, inspiration for Demonic Christianity, but which, ironically, best expresses its revolutionary hope. My theme was the Hope, the eschatology of Marxism, a veritable secularization of Revelation. I taught Engels, Kautsky, Ernst Bloch, the "Marxist- Christian dialogue" and Moltmann's *A Theology of Hope*. In Hope, inspired by the vision of theistic Jesus and of atheistic Marx, irrepressible Spirit is there, "something happening," transforming History.

I quit College and went back to Church

By my last Vassar year I was being nagged by my natal calling—the Church. I left Church mad, in the ecstasy of wrenching conversions. Church had baptized me wrong, nourished, nurtured and sent me passionately down wrong paths. Most people on the wrong side seemed to be from Church. Excepting Black Movement churches, the secular Anti-Vietnam Movement and its Students had more commitment to social justice than to church. For the first time in my wrenched-around life I found myself in what seemed a seamless community of secular leftists, and found initiation there more Grace-filled than my religion. I indignantly quit Church and went to academia.

Eleven years later, however, things had changed. Students, no longer threatened by the draft, were uninterested in the public sphere. Faculty colleagues with whom I'd shared the barricades had failed to get tenure and left, or had obtained it and joined the other side. Ironically, most of the few who were still engaged had turned out to be closet Christians or Jews. Finally, I was fired from a liberal college for my alleged radicalism.

After eleven years the prophetic mantle had passed from academia. On at least some major issues, at least a corner of the prophetic mantle was being picked up by liberal churches. Also, I'd begun to notice some things. After four years under my ministry, students not only left to scatter across the round belly of the earth, but considered the day of their leaving the proudest and gladdest of moments. Colleagues in the churches, by contrast, had folks who'd been born and would die in their church. They presided over births, deaths and marriages of their people, every age and many different walks of life. They engaged people in a far wider spectrum of life issues, and guided institutions where much more was at stake than in the little chaplain's office.

I began to wonder about going back to church, going not on my religious "head," but on my revolutionary "feet." The reality, though, was that I had a miserable record in the Church and couldn't even survive in liberal academia. It seemed a pipe dream. Nonetheless, I made a list of fifty people who were successful and influential in liberal denominations and went to see them. I gave as honest an assessment as I could of my gifts, my leftist commitments, my sorry history, my anger at the church upon leaving, and my interest in returning.

What were my chances? Most essentially patted me on the head, told me I'd do fine and not to worry about it, that it's a waste of time. With one, only one, exception. George Younger was parent to two of my students. He'd attended chapel on visits and seemed appreciative. He was Executive Minister of American Baptist Churches in New Jersey. I arrived first thing one morning and spent the day with him. He had me talk about my anger at the church, about how I saw my leftist commitments at play in a potential ministry, how I'd handle church opposition. A lot of questions. Relentless follow-up. Hours of it. Late in the afternoon he said I couldn't make it in any ABC church in New Jersey. There were, however, three churches currently open elsewhere where I might succeed. He'd recommend me. I indeed heard from all three, and in fairly short order accepted the call to one of them: First Baptist Church of Granville, Ohio. So, I quit college and went back to church.

In a way, I was excited to have a job and be back in a church, but after the unique position I'd held in an elite college, the thrill of moral leadership in the prophetic Seventies, the eagerness and enthusiasm of my students, this felt like another failure and a significant comedown. Tiny town, middle America, the second smallest of seven churches in town, an aging congregation in modest decline. And I was forty-one years old.

What happened in Granville, however, was something else altogether, and is the occasion for this memoir.

Uprisings in Middle America

During my first Easter in Granville I gave a series of lectures on Mary Magdalene. My Mary was abused, victimized by religion and Jesus Movement men, angry, lashing out. Afterward, Barbara Klatt, sobbing rage, attacked my religion on Mary's behalf, blaming me, the messenger.

She cried old angers and new, like sexist language in hymns and liturgies. So we formed a worship committee, similar to the Chapel Board at Vassar. Identifying other feminists, including my wife, Carol, and my staff colleague, Julie Galambush, she started a Sunday discussion and a support group. I was surrounded, as if the decade-old Feminist Movement was born again, this time religious, local, at church, office, home. No one was ever the same.

There evolved the Feminist Sunday School Class, including women from other churches and no churches. They read feminism erupting in books, young writers battering doors of seminaries, spewing heresies—angry anti-religious ones as well. Suddenly this Baptist church was awash in author names and mind-bending quotations. Those not in the class were too intimidated by their charisma to say a word. Vassar, the feminist institution, was nothing like this. In the class, the Wicca Circle, ancient Goddess-worship rituals, Solstice and croning celebrations, the labyrinth they built and taught us to walk, three support groups— the women of Granville seized the day like nothing I've seen in serial collisions with social movements. I was particularly blessed by intense friendships with these women, especially Karolyn Burkett, charismatic leader of the Granville movement and matriarch of the sprawling Burkett family compound. Karolyn knew, learned and taught me the full spectrum, including the spiritual dimension, of what it is to be human in a bi-gender world.

We husbands formed a support group—for survival. Wives were clearing social space we'd occupied, for themselves, using metaphors, images, whole languages opaque to us. They were powerful, alien, angry at, among many other objects, us. We needed each other, to tend bruises and give reassurance to wounded egos. We were also their chief admirers.

Alien to movement spirit, we wanted what they'd found. If we were to retain self-respect, we couldn't go on as before. As a function of their movement, we revised our ways of being men. There was shame, as with my racism, but we had each other to share it with, laugh with—the human comedy. Our wives would host their group in our homes, and we would host ours in theirs—spouses banished to nether domestic regions. We spun a myth that Women's Group cried, and Men's Group laughed. Though I live a quarter-continent distant from those men, we still meet at least a weekend every year. The women charged the church into a movement of its own, spinning off explosive projects for us men and other women. One they kept. In assault on Right to Life politics, they adopted a local organization offering access to abortion for women without financial or social means.

THE RELIGIOUS RIGHT

If there is a social movement in which I had significant leadership through forces beyond my intention, it's the Peace Movement. Not because I was from a liberal, sophisticated Student Movement chaplaincy. It was because of my conservative, fundamentalist Southern Baptist roots, the most warmongering of backgrounds.

Peace activism became a movement with the Reagan presidency. His Cold War belligerence, intemperate nuclear armament, and his stepchild, the Religious Right Movement set it off. Many understood the former two better than I, but I recognized with horror the potential of the New Right religious passion. White liberal activists hadn't a clue, didn't take it seriously. For me, exposing and combating the Religious Right became a mission.

The Religious Right was the first reactionary social movement after Civil Rights, seen in my quirky history as its dark twin. Both were biblical, based on the Exodus, led by preachers and organized by churches. For King, the Exodus was the first nonviolent social revolution, a miraculous freeing of slaves. The Right celebrates the catastrophic plagues, death of Egypt's firstborn, drowning of its army, Holy War genocide against "infidels," and elevating the Abrahamic tradition as the "people of God." More fateful was their twin take on the Jesus Movement. King saw it as liberation. The Right saw it as Apocalypse—War of the Lamb; the final Holy War waged by the Church with Jesus its head, against the world; and the "Rapture," Christians swept into Heaven, leaving everyone else to burn forever in the "Lake of Fire."

This I understood, because I had only recently believed it myself. My colleagues, movement chaplains and pastors, either never believed or rejected it with contempt. They (and for a time, I) simply proclaimed The Right to be wrong and preached the Prophets and Sermon on the Mount, as if the rest of Scripture were merely background noise. That would change, but even then I read the religion of The Right from the inside and foresaw the disaster toward which it headed. I also understood it as a social movement, having been bowled over by six of them.

Karen Armstrong's *The Battle for God* helped me see that this movement was worldwide, soon to manifest, to be called, after, ironically, a movement of twentieth century American Protestant Fundamentalists everywhere (fundamentalist Catholics of Northern Ireland, Jews of Palestine, Hindus of India, Orthodox of Serbia, and Muslim Jihadists). The Right's "Moses" was Jerry Falwell, a Baptist preacher like Dr. King—and me. His Moral Majority, like Fundamentalists everywhere, saw themselves a majority bullied by a secular elite. They believed the Left to be atheist, wanting everyone to be atheist. The U.N., a proto "world government," was Anti-Christ forecast in The Book of Revelation. The Peace Movement sabotaged the War of the Lamb, God's apocalyptic end to History, whose sword was the Hydrogen Bomb, whose army was America.

Falwell wasn't eloquent or typically charismatic. Reagan was. Though unreligious, a true Machiavellian, he brandished apocalyptic ideology as if he were. He held contempt for "unpatriotic" war protesters, "godless communist" critics of capitalist excess, "women's libber" careerists forsaking the "sacred American family," sexual libertines on the pill, abortions, "the homosexual lifestyle" its "homosexual agenda" to turn us all gay, "welfare cheats" who "won't work," and "long-haired hippies." His "Southern Strategy," as Lyndon Johnson predicted with passage of civil rights legislation, was simply to champion "States Rights." Republicans carried the South for the first time since Reconstruction. He added Machiavellian biblical terms to his populist oratory ("God," "Christ," "divinely-ordained destiny," "abomination," "Evil Empire") and graciously donned the mantle of divinely-bestowed power.

BAPTIST PEACE FELLOWSHIP OF NORTH AMERICA

The Student Movement had petered out, my job destroyed. Two years later, upended yet again, without meaning to or being aware of what was happening, I became founding president of an international Peace organization that would be the largest, most active among its Protestant peers.

I had joined Ohio American Baptists, a Yankee denomination Southerners had abandoned for the Civil War. Ohio Baptist executive John Sundquist, of my new congregation, asked me—the new liberal—to gather the few Ohio Baptist peace activists. I did, and was chosen leader. My church had no history of peace work and had Vietnam vets and fundamentalists in leadership. My focus wasn't peace. It was rather how much catch-up I needed on church leadership skills, and how much uphill my liberal commitments had to climb.

Still, we found a hundred other Nuclear Freeze supporters who wanted to act, and our meetings stirred movement excitement. We made such a stir that the Right organized against us. Before the Ohio Baptist Convention meeting I was called on to debate a fundamentalist who blasted us for siding with the Anti-Christ against the apocalyptic advent of God's Millennium.

The 1983 American Baptist convention was held in Ohio. We had enough steam behind us to get on the program. There was a denominational Peace Fellowship, a forty-year-old association of pacifists who mimeographed a newsletter and held breakfasts at conventions. They invited us to the breakfast. Someone moved they adopt a board structure "and become activist like these Ohio peaceniks." His proposal accepted, he was nominated president, but he was being fired from his church for being too liberal, couldn't accept, and nominated me. I said, "I'm not a member." They joined me to the Association and elected "the new guy from Ohio" president. The program was a group who'd gone on a peace mission to the Soviet Union. They'd been joined by Southern

Baptists who were interested in pursuing "association with us."

I followed up and found that these southerners had done more in a couple years than our group had in forty. I proposed exploring a relationship. "Never!" said the liberal Yankees who had only contempt for Southern Baptists. But as one myself I said that among thirty million there were hundreds like me. My tales of alienation in the tiny liberal remnant "down there" made resonance with them who were alienated "up here." We set a meeting with them.

It was one of those spark-to-oil happenings from which movements come. In three days' raucous dreaming, flinging caution to the wind, we formed the Baptist Peace Fellowship of North America, because as "citizens of The Beast" we needed to bring in the continent. As the one Southern/American Baptist who as such had pulled the meeting off, I was elected President. The Vice President and half the board were Southerners, a cacophony of accents, in other words, Pentecost. We left hysterical, committed to freeze nukes, end the Cold War, and transform America's largest Protestant church into a Peace Church.

Within months we had Mexicans, Canadians, Puerto Ricans and half of the dozen splintered Baptist denominations in our Free Church tradition. We had no money, but without staff couldn't accomplish anything. At the second meeting, the new VP roomed with me. We stayed up, getting acquainted, drinking whiskey. He proposed quitting his job to become our exec. He had skills and contacts to raise enough to pay himself and justify the office. We and a couple bottles of Jack Daniels lasted the night, and by early morning had a plan. Bleary-eyed, we presented it to the board, who said, "why-the-hell-not?"

Ken Sehested became charismatic leader of a new Baptist social movement, upending me yet again. Next summer we held the first of, so far, thirty week-long movement gatherings, several hundred Baptist peaceniks, all ages, "part peace conference, part revival." Guess what we sang? Children from the first ten Peace Camps, now adults, compose half the board.

Ken became my closest friend. Now in his seventh decade, he's lived a life of radical activism, more so than any I know. We saw social movement whirlwinds from their vortex, hurled to unlikely places, met a chaos of charismatic leaders and movement multitudes around the world.

I preached at First Baptist Moscow, Cold War, first Sunday, Russian Christianity's thousandth year, three thousand standing shoulder-to-shoulder; at Tokyo Peace Church and First Baptist, Managua, "Amazing Grace" in Russian, Japanese and Spanish; served communion in a Bangkok hotel to guerrilla leaders of the Myanmar insurgency, maps and AK47s on the bed; visited, his home and mine, Gustavo Parajon from Central America's largest relief and development movement; plotted in Sweden with revolutionaries from six continents; met in Moscow homes of Perestroika dissidents, recently released from the Gulag; with Daniel Ortega on a truck bed before thousands in red bandanas, Sandinista Revolution's tenth anniversary; visited the Warsaw home of Solidarity's Communication Minister; committed civil disobedience against the US Navy at Vieques Island, Puerto Rico; saw subversive papers mimeographed in an East Berlin church; stood in a Seoul, Korea student protest; wandered the war-torn streets of Belfast; preached to a convocation of Latin American Communists, introduced and translated by a Sandinista.

With Doug Donley I took a protest swim in a Nicaragua harbor blockaded by US mines. A friend photographed me emerging from the water in jockey shorts and delivered it to my kids who sent it on a Christmas card to our card list, saying, "Dad makes us pose for Christmas pictures every year. Here's Dad. Love, Peter, Dan and Chris."

Twenty-five years later, my friend Paul Dekar, a Canadian historian, wrote the history of the Peace Fellowship's first quarter -century. He lifts from the Religious Right Baptist mainstream the multifaceted reality of our movement. Its stories of social force threaded with vignettes of roughly three hundred individuals drawn by movement power, most of them my friends, many as wrenched around as me, achieving far more in the clamor toward Peace. Nothing is more thrilling than three decades of Movement community with these heroes. Grace.

It wasn't really Uncle Jack, Loebl or the Bolsheviks who got me in an actual socialist revolution. It was First Baptist Church of Granville, its favorite son Gustavo Parajon and the Sandinistas. Gus was student pastor in the church while attending college at Denison University across the street. He married in the church, and after medical school went back to his native Nicaragua. By the time I met him, he was pastor of First Baptist Church of Managua, head of a medical-dental service organization that worked with the poorest people in the most primitive areas, and founder of CEPAD, Central America's most influential relief and development movement. Gus was in the revolution, and though a Protestant and not a party member, had won the respect of the Catholic Sandinista cadre. CEPAD became the de facto service arm of the government.

Gus became chief advocate for Miskito Indians with whom the Sandinistas pursued an otherwise disastrous policy. Throughout Reagan's counter-revolutionary Contra war against the Sandinistas, Gus was regularly in the US and Europe speaking for the revolution, against the war, and having the widest and most receptive hearing of pro-revolution Nicaraguans. Among most anti-communist Baptist colleagues, he was considered a godless Marxist and vilified. In Nicaragua he was number one on the Contra hit list. Every week he did medical work in the jungles, and he had to travel with a bodyguard. I was often there when he returned from his weekly ministry to dancing celebration by his congregation. With him and the Sandinistas I met students from Nicaragua's revolutionary Literacy Campaign. He showed me a crucifixion scene, Jesus' disciples identifiable as the Sandinista Cadre. Of the "Great Ones" I've know personally, Gus is by far the greatest.

A Communist couple came to church. She was baptized— as a Communist—finding our church more committed to social transformation than to the opiate of the masses. With these beautiful people I saw the workings of the American Communist Party renovating structures which disenfranchised laborers. And I got the basics on Marxist analysis of contemporary reality.

Environmental Revolution, Work Abuse, Empire and Goddamned Christians

Throughout twenty-three years in Granville I continued being upended. It's humiliating to write this, but since it is the point of the book, it must be done.

I was shocked with shame when the Environmental Movement confronted the scandal of my footprint: the out-sized volume of carbon spilled from my excesses, precious nonrenewable resources used up forever, the indestructible trash. If a quarter of humanity were to tread with my footprint across the human landscape, life as we know it would cease to be possible. What distraction diverted my conscience from this impact? What spiritual vacuum left me with such appetites? Until environmental activists spelled it out, I had no idea. I never hurt anybody making my footprint: flushing toilets too much, burning bulbs too watted, too long; shutting spigots too hot, too little; inhabiting too many resource-gobbling, pollution-spewing cubic feet, then way too many, and finally an obscenity of them; driving, flying and speed-boating too much too far; neglecting too long the greener alternatives.

It now appears that in the wastelands of the distant future, when our genocides, bigotries and exploitations are forgotten, the dread Evil from our century still remembered and cursed will be what we did to the Earth, and left undone. And most of it will have been done, and neglected, by the likes of me.

Also, my church job was a pious excuse for workaholism. I avoided this diagnosis until I found in a bolt of horror my absence in the experience of my kids. The image we clergy project is of selfless service to God and neighbor. Bullshit! I was at least as proud, ambitious, focused on advancement, and addicted as any greedy corporate lawyer. I craved flattering feedback, spent hours earning it, surplus hours getting more. I actually worked at being controversial and even despised: the image, you know, of integrity, prophetic courage. Abandoning myself, I became my work and the image I struggled to project.

The only things I didn't work at were spiritual disciplines of integrity, spiritual identity and trust—which I taught. I inflated the importance of myself and my work way out of proportion. How much more valuable it would have been to spend an extra hour a day with Carol and the kids. It would have added a year to my time with them. A year! But for work abuse I might have been a fuller, realer presence for my people, a better example. Just being there for them, I wouldn't have needed the enemies list I'm about to describe. Nor would I have fallen asleep in counseling sessions a half-dozen times. Being my workaholic daddy's kid, I had no idea.

Of all my demonic "-isms," workaholism is the only one from which I fully recovered. In my late fifties I decided to retire at sixty-five. But I "loved my work," couldn't imagine myself apart from it, suffered panic attacks about prospects of empty hours and existential death.

One day I heard myself say, "I dread this meeting." Being so repressed I hadn't meant to say that, but it was true. I did dread it, and in three more years I would never have to go to such a meeting again. The liberating pilgrimage which began that day was a three- year grousing about dark closets in the innards of my professional life for other things I didn't like. Turns out, there was a bunch. Upon finding them, I embraced each one, celebrated, and added to the growing list of all I wouldn't ever have to do again. And, I must say, however much I may have failed at in ministry, after nearly a decade of retirement, I'm succeeding rather well at that.

And Empire. 9/11, more than any single day, turned me all the way over. That Sunday Rev. Jeremiah Wright preached his "chickens home to roost" sermon, the most vilified in recent American homiletics, which his parishioner, Barack Obama, was forced by political necessity to condemn. That same day I preached a strikingly similar sermon, to be published in a 9/11 collection. Dan, our political comic, bragged that were he to run for office, he'd have to renounce me.

Terrorism is a strategy employed by the very weak and desperate against the very powerful and secure. Its goal is to provoke a great power to expose its worst to a watching world. By contrast, for a few days in New York City, 9/11 brought out America's best—the hope in our two sermons. But the terrorist strategy ultimately worked. For succeeding years the American Empire unsheathed from its revolutionary scabbard the demonic in its swift sword, bloodied the world with hate, and jerked from peoples everywhere—from me—an unanswerable outcry against red-blooded American Evil.

During these years, with the help of Bible scholar friends, I plummeted into a most depressing discovery. The Bible is from beginning to end set against one overriding manifestation of Evil. Empire! First the Egyptian, then Persian, and finally Roman Empire, none of which had in their day anything like the world-hegemonic power the American Empire has in ours. The American Empire has more cultural domination, weapons of mass destruction, vehicles for lethal delivery, technological agility, budgetary capacity, more planetary reach and extra-planetary military positions than all other nations combined. America, which first developed weapons of mass destruction, is for two generations the only ever to unleash them on urban populations. It has enough of them cocked for immediate attack to destroy all life.

This is my country, land that I love, who in this world I am. Being born in "the land of the free and the home of the brave" identifies me with the American Empire. Whatever patriots and presidential candidates might say, for more than half the world this is prime evidence of my fallenness. Until turned over by 9/11, I had no idea.

After a youth spent romanticizing Christians, in 1962 I entered their employ. Talk about upended! For the next forty-two years my central life struggle was to survive professionally among them. In nine months I was fired from my fieldwork job, nearly fired from my first church job, was spectacularly fired from my third, barely escaped being fired midway through my fourth, and finally was ejected, along with my whole church, from our denomination.

In extravagant de-sacralization, Martin Luther said no priest, indeed no Pope had any more Calling from God than the meanest housewife, burgomaster, soldier or hangman. Nonetheless, we professional holy types never gave up the claim that God sets us uniquely aside for sacred vocation. Nearly all my colleagues talk about their bruising struggles up the ecclesiastical ladder as arranged and revealed in gut-wrenching prayer by God, as if God cared which church your average reverend had, any more than which bank your average capitalist had—a professional narcissism reserved entirely for clergy.

I thought the same before my first firing. In subsequent years I've had to reconcile the fact that the people I've disliked most, obsessed most lethally about, and schemed most to defeat have been a few Christians I've had to work for and with. I have here on my writing desk a list of their names, forty-two years' worth. To publish it with candid caricatures would be so very therapeutic. On the other hand, the very existence of the list; the anger and hatred it arouses; the vignettes of my phoniness, hypocrisy, meanness and sheer failure in relationship is one of my more disappointing symptoms of bad character.

To these I add the ways and times I reduced my job to a merely instrumental and self-serving missile aimed at their defeat. I was, after all, their pastor, entrusted with the care of their souls, or their colleague in a mission which they doubtless found as difficult as I did.

Having been Born, Born Again, I had no idea.

CARL UPCHURCH

Carl didn't turn me upside down. He drew me up short. He had a charisma, physical presence, personal winsomeness to fill rooms and snatch the breath from adoring audiences. Once, perusing my bookshelf, he drew a classic, then another, and without opening either quoted paragraphs from memory. He had more potential than anyone I've known. He had a mission.

Carl was black; he spent most of his first thirty years in prison, and the rest in a ghetto, beset by a host of demons. Though brilliant, until he was discovered by Quaker prison workers he couldn't read. By an unlikely twist of fate for the last quarter of his life I was Carl's pastor. I performed his wedding, dedicated his children, spent hours counseling him, and many hours in pursuit of his calling with him. Mostly, though, I failed with Carl. I was way beyond my depth.

By the time I met him he'd founded a self-help movement among fellow inmates. He penetrated the iron curtain of prison wardens and despite being an excluded ex-inmate secured a meager redemptive presence in several institutions. They believed in him and were committed to his movement.

His concept was exceptional. What he didn't have was income, and not a clue about organization, fundraising or managing a budget. There were a dozen ways I could help get him up and running, and I did. Within months he was on speaking tours, visiting prisons, conducting phone interviews with inmates from an office at church. A national peace and justice organization bestowed on Carl its highest honor and we hired a managing director. Then his demons erupted, this exceptional genius self-destructed, and we shut it all down.

After a time, former inmate clients in warring west coast gangs asked Carl to mediate their conflict. We got funding and he effected something of a miracle. He was back in our church office getting calls through our switchboard from Crips and Bloods with dreadful handles. I found a prominent Kansas City pastor who helped him organize a national summit of warring gang leaders—the first of its kind. It did some good, more because of the pastor and others than Carl. By the time of the meeting, Carl was in the grip of his demons again.

My growing anger, diminishing contribution to his welfare and his increasing awareness of ambiguities in our friendship finally sabotaged it. He got a job with the state working in the ghetto. His autobiography got significant national distribution, doing more good among ghetto youth, ex-inmates and others than I've done in my lifetime. But he died young, strangled by his demons, leaving a young family in grief, never getting within leagues of his promise.

Preparation for Carl's hugely attended funeral dragged me through my wasted landscape of failures: to earn sufficient trust, invest enough time or take the tough risks of genuine friendship. A eulogy is no place for confession, but the inwardness of my public oratory made tortuous settlement with my worst.

I loved Carl, and used him; was demonically proud of Carl, and proud of myself as his advocate; got past my racism with Carl, and exorcised it at his expense; accompanied Carl through the exploration of his soul as pastor, and voyeur; admired Carl's enormous power, and, abdicating responsibility, dreaded it; sacrificed for Carl, and exploited him; gave him my best, and siphoned his best for my own end. I spent time of intense quality with him, and abandoned him. I was at my best with Carl, sabotaging him with my flawed best. The positive poles of these ambiguities were active and deliberate, what I did. What I did was an expression of Grace. The negative were largely passive, who I am.

Who I am, as the old theology would have it, is the "Image of God," which is already ambiguous. But what I really am is the Image of God ambiguously, or more to the point, paradoxically. I am the Image of God, spoiled. We'll get to this.

"George has fallen again"

Hiking with Peter, I fell—again. Peter heard my putative last words, "Oh shit!" I landed in a granite creek bed, crushing heel, ankle and femur. Alien blood from the first fall proving insufficient, I had hematological problems, keeping me horizontal a couple months. Cliff told me after the second fall, twenty-five years after the first, his sister Peggy phoned him to say, "George has fallen again." I fall a lot. The first reorganized my face and hematology; the second, my life. Had it not, I wouldn't be writing a memoir.

Two things happened, first at Peace Camp, a beloved community where Peter and I were headed. I was at—get this—Transylvania Hospital, appropriately, losing blood count. My surgeon, with the bedside manner of Dracula, implied I was failing. Back at camp, Peter got emotional with these grim suspicions. So Baptists gathered in prayer—for me. A conferee, actually Dracula's medical partner, intervened. Through him and the prayers I recovered— Amazing Grace—but I convalesced for a month.

Coincidentally, forces from the right of the Granville church were gathering to get me fired—again. The church had a lopsided power structure, dominated by three families whose wealth and influence overshadowed the rank and file. They'd run off several of my predecessors. Early on, when my political bent became clear, these patriarchs gave me a severe warning, but many of their fellow conservatives had fled. (There was a modest group of new radicals, groupies of mine.) Though their influence had diminished, the patriarchs set wheels in motion to send me packing, but my fall sent shock waves through the congregation that set them back. In the shock's wake, the progressives decided to take over. Riding a wave of sympathy for the wounded pastor, they succeeded. By the time I limped back to the pulpit, the shaken-down congregation was ready to take on the world. In the ensuing turbulence of Grace, we did— resulting in, among other things, this memoir. The Amazing Grace guy is also the guy who falls a lot—metaphorically as well as actually.

IRAQ

Just before the outbreak of the first Gulf War, the Fellowship of Reconciliation (FOR) gathered a group of activists to go on what turned out to be the only peace mission to Iraq. Since I would be gone during Advent, I asked for the church's okay. "GO," they said.

The US embargo, just instituted, little affected the Iraqi government, but was catastrophic for citizens, especially children. So we took three tons of medicine to the Saddam Children's Hospital in Baghdad. Just before leaving, I received a late night call from someone claiming to be from the State Department. He said if I were to make this illegal embargo-bust I would be slapped with a "ruinous" fine and "possible prison term." I checked with FOR, who said no one else got such a bizarre call, and not to take it seriously. I didn't.

My knowledge of Mideast history was zilch. I crammed a crash course, then flew to Amman, grilling colleagues for what they knew. We engaged Jordanian and Palestinian intellectuals from whom I heard mind-bending facts and sizzling opinions. By the time our charter touched down (the one plane that day at Baghdad International) and we stepped into its cavernous hall with our medicine, I was throbbing with adrenaline and stimulation.

Our arrival, visits with hospital kids and presentation of medicine were on TV. Everywhere we were hailed, offered gifts. Before leaving Granville, Tom Burkett had photographed our church children and given me pocketfuls of snapshots. These I gave to kids at the hospital and schools—to squeals of delight.

I took a lone pilgrimage to Baghdad University, where I was sent to the English Department for folks fluent in my language. It was in the division for traditional Muslim women, who wore head-scarves. Faculty had studied at Ivy League and Chicago, and one, like me, at Vanderbilt. They were a delight. They laughed at my political questions, saying I wouldn't find any student willing to speak to me.

I was directed to the student cafeteria, where I got attention just by walking in. I shouted an invitation to English talkers and a couple dozen descended noisily on a table for half that. One was from Kuwait, who'd fled after the invasion. I asked about the Iraqi occupation. Into a deathly silence of her peers she boldly said, "It's wrong!" I immediately regretted asking—no telling what consequences she may have faced. "Could we study in America?" "Could we wear the scarf?" Of course. I told about Ohio State, where traditional Muslims abound. They asked if I had kids. They snatched and exclaimed over the photos. From behind scarves they pronounced my sons "hot!"

We visited American workers housed in the American Embassy. They were "detainees," to be "human shields" against US bombing. April Glaspie, US Ambassador, after giving tacit US blessing on the proposed invasion of Kuwait, had left the country. We collected messages from detainees for their families. A member of our visiting group revealed that, unbeknownst to FOR, he worked for the same company as some of them. He met privately with them. As ours was a peace mission, we were concerned about his intentions.

I was chosen to ride herd on him. He somehow had access to Muhammad Ali, also seeking detainees' release. Our guy arranged to visit Ali, so I went. There he was in the doorway to his room, the great man in his robe. He did a few of his famous magic tricks for us and the cleaning women hanging by his door. He was busy, but invited us for breakfast.

Seared on the cortex of my memory is the image of the most recognizable man on earth, the sheer power and beauty of him blowing through the lobby of Al Rasheed Hotel, the very definition of charisma, Arab eyes wide, mouths agape at this hero who'd given up his name and religion to become a Muslim, little me at his side, trailed by videographers, cameras rolling. Two days later Ali liberated the detainees, taking them home with him, and our rogue, my charge, in tow, their picture on the front of every paper on the planet.

We visited Tariq Aziz, Saddam's vice president, the regime's anomalous Christian, joined by Lakota Indians who'd somehow made it round the world without passports or much money. A lanky, wizened shaman, the Pipe Keeper, performed a peace-pipe ceremony. He lit an ancient long stem pipe and had each of us, Aziz included, inhale, breathe out and watch the smoke evaporate. This, he said, would eventually envelop the planet to be inhaled into the life force of every living being. We, and all of humanity, were in that ceremony, one. In twenty years Aziz would be sentenced to death by the Iraqi High Tribune, a sentence commuted to life in the wake of international protest.

On the first Sunday in Advent I found an Anglican church. The sanctuary was a monument to the holiness of war and sanctity of warriors. Windows, pews, and altar were dedicated to Her Majesty's this or that regiment or officer, who was dispatched to wreak havoc in "Arabia" and to worship the God of Jesus in a Muslim neighborhood. It was the opening Advent hymn that sent me packing. Despite the glorious seventy-degree cloudless day, the same latitude and a scant hundred miles from Bethlehem, there went up the sort of drone only Anglicans can make, to—I kid you not—"In the bleak midwinter!"

Our last day there, in what was surely the grandest thing I ever did, I caused a subversive ruckus among a thousand Iraqi children at an official ceremony—a story I'll save for the book's end. Returning home to enormous media coverage, I was granted further leave by the church for seventy anti-war speeches, coast to coast. Other churches in town and most everywhere sprouted yellow pro-war ribbons and proud American flags. Two weeks later Tom Burkett called and said to turn on my TV—the bombing of Baghdad.

TWO BIBLES

I've known two Bibles. There was one at church, and the other re-imagined and laughed at with Cliff. Both, of course, folded between the same leather "Holy Bible" covers. I eventually chose one over the other.

Figuring this out began with the Secularization materials. First were the irrefutable contradictions of core biblical "truths," cosmic "truths" challenged by Galileo and Darwin, moral "truths" debunked by Machiavelli and Marx. Then there were the mere biblical refutations by giants of the Church and Christian academia. Anthropology depicted the universality of religion, the thirty thousand known humanly constructed religions, each more bizarre than the last, none more so than sections of the Bible. All this came to me as my own ethical and spiritual challenges grew ever more complicated and costly.

Then the Iraq visit. A Palestinian intellectual brought up the Crusades, "the genocide of my people for your War God," he said. He quoted from a worn Bible, reading to me "nine divine mandates to 'expel,' 'enslave,' and 'slaughter' to the last woman and child the indigenous people of this land—my people," he said. He closed with Deuteronomy 20: "Thus says YHWH: As for the towns of these peoples that YHWH your God is giving you, you must not let anything that breathes remain alive. You shall annihilate them just as YHWH your God has commanded ..." or face worse from YHWH themselves.

I went home, secured a sabbatical, and spent it with what Marcion in the second century called an "evil Bible of an evil God," for which he was condemned. For him, it was Hebrew Scriptures. Crusaders' Evil passages were, rather, from both testaments. Crusader interpretations were more or less right. It is all there. Chief among Crusader sources is the Psalms, known by illiterate worshipers from singing them in the mass. Two-thirds of the Psalms are war songs celebrating battles of God's people against their "enemies" and God's—the people of the land, the land being modern Palestine. War is a major "holy" theme in the Bible, sometimes under God's command, sometimes apocalyptic violence from God alone. Much Scripture is hate-filled, condemning the enemies of God by God or God's people. The language is xenophobic.

Many texts, including many I had memorized, command separation of God's people from racial others—legislating oppressive treatment and slavery, cited in pro-slavery/segregation tracts and sermons. As they all emphasize, nothing in all the Bible is explicitly critical of slavery or racial segregation.

During my sabbatical my church and I were under biblical condemnation for being gay-friendly. Biblical Christians were wreaking havoc among LGBTQ people. Seven biblical texts quoted in tracts and news articles called for church exclusion, persecution, and even execution—the Bible using the same hate-filled emotional language of the worst homophobes.

The Feminist Class taught me Phyllis Trible's *Texts of Terror,* five biblical stories of ghastly female brutalization done by biblical "patriarchs." The Law of God, addressed only to propertied males, is blatantly misogynist. While Paul declares Christians "freed from the Law," he piously retains its misogyny.

Though written by and for Jews, the Prophetic books are bitter in their condemnation of Israel, their own country, for its apostasy—texts adopted by centuries of anti-Semites. The Gospel writers blame "the Jews" for the crucifixion of Jesus—as opposed to the Romans, whose favor they were courting. Paul, an intensely observant Jew, became increasingly vindictive toward his people, excoriating "the Jews" for rejecting his message. Martin Luther was the first great biblical scholar of Christian history. His anti-Semitism draws from and permeates his exegesis, bequeathing it to the ages.

And so on.

I grew up knowing these passages. If I had occasion to question their morality, my teachers would quote Isaiah 55:9f,

"My thoughts are not your thoughts . . . says YHWH. As the heavens are higher than the earth, so are . . . my thoughts higher than your thoughts." In other words, don't think about it. This admonition delayed my moral reasoning a decade. I began moral critique of Scripture on sabbatical, identifying the Bible's Religious Evil, religion on the wrong side, people doing terrible things as Calling from God, with the whole heart.

But religious evil was not all I studied. I who loved biblical Religious Evil was later wrenched around, repeatedly, only to meet the Bible on the other side. Scripture inspired the Torquemadas, but also the Martin Luther Kings. I read about biblical people who did profound good. They all knew and were inspired by the great biblical social movements: the Hebrew prophetic uprising, the Jesus uprising, the Jerusalem church. These were my "GREAT ONES:" The Friars Minor, Jan Hus, Protestant Reformers, Quakers, Shakers, Diggers and Levellers, abolitionists, Nat Turner, Harriet Tubman, Wilberforce, Gandhi, King, Fannie Lou Hamer, Mother Teresa, and contemporary great ones.

Arguing with the Bible is one thing. Arguing with Fundamentalist pastors is something else. What they have (they don't admit it) is a "hermeneutic"—professional jargon for "method of interpretation." Theirs is to credit the whole damned thing. Responding to their absolutes with "But that's not my experience" doesn't cut it. What I needed was a hermeneutic to separate GREAT ONES' grains of biblical wheat from truckloads of biblical chaff.

Biblical hermeneutics is a cacophony of often bitterly competing alternatives. This is why the old Church kept the Bible in Latin, so plain folks couldn't read and interpret Scripture. The Church did it for them. By contrast, Baptists have said any fool can read it as well as the next. I'm Baptist. There is no "right" method, but given the Bible's role in centuries of Religious Evil, given that Jesus and Hebrew tradition say the "whole law" is summed up by "Love your neighbor," there are plenty of "wrong" ones.

First step toward a hermeneutic is identifying the Two Bibles.

Much recommends the redemptive passages. Gandhi was inspired by Jesus on Love, Justice and Peace, King by Justice in the Prophets, Love in Deuteronomy and Jesus, Peace in Jesus and Isaiah, and by Hope in Jesus and Revelation. Liberationists see God among the oppressed in both testaments. Nat Turner followed Moses' revolt of slaves. My Anabaptists, barely literate, wrestling out a word at a time, could make out the whole Sermon on the Mount, the Bible's defining summary.

But what's wrong with the rest? Why is it in there? How do I use it?

Over time I identified the locus and character of the two Bibles. The longer one I call "Priestcraft" Bible, focused on religion, worship, sacred history of the religion, and a concept of spiritual "cleanness" or "holiness." Holiness is opposite "defilement," "blemish" and "abomination." Its focus is otherworldly and its goal is eternal salvation of the individual. Priestcraft demands inwardness and keeping God's Law, a totemic law, marking not morality per se, but membership in the community of God's people—like my Not-Dancing. God's Law is the rules and heroic history of Religious Evil. It contains words of religious comfort, spectacles of religious celebration. It is esoteric, a matter not of mind but of revelation and absolute belief. It is very long and detailed. It is Bible as officially followed by the Church. It is not Evil per se. It includes everything useful for religion and spiritual practice, and it organizes these, not according to the Prophetic, but to Religious Evil. From the point of view of the Prophetic Bible, it presents and advocates Religion and spirituality as Evil.

The other, learned from Mac and the GREAT ONES, is "Prophetic" Bible: eighth-century prophets (Amos, Hosea, Isaiah, Micah, Jeremiah and Second Isaiah) and Synoptic Gospels (Matthew, Mark, Luke and John) minus birth narratives; also Ruth, Job, Song of Songs, Jonah, Acts, James and Revelation 21. It is radically critical of religion, often anti-religious, focused on this world, God's "good" Creation. Its goal is redemptive transformation of History. Not detailed in directives, it is open to unforeseen circumstances, unimagined moral directions. A redemptive response is left to be rationally determined, but from one principle—"Good News for the Poor" (Jesus and Second Isaiah). It inspires, not Church, but the "Prophetic Remnant."

In the Prophetic Bible, Religion and inner spirituality are not Evil per se. Both are practiced by some of its characters, but it offers absolutely nothing on either. It therefore must be supplemented by the Priestcraft Bible, but reorganized by a prophetic commitment.

The Soul of Social Movements

In my lumpy life's most fateful event, the Sit-in, I was capsized by a social movement. It gave me a new totem, the old one (Not-Dancing-For-God) having been lost in the dancing on campus social movement. Ignorant of social movements, I tucked both beneath my repressions and got on with life. But it happened again, then serially. I would become the movement's doormat, its butt, patsy, wrenched repeatedly around.

By the time of my Two Bibles sabbatical, I was consumed with the LGBTQ uprising and biblical homophobia. I had been swallowed into the LGBTQ Movement at Vassar. What reawakened me to it was AIDS. Churches were proclaiming AIDS to be God's vindictive doing. So I joined a few modestly out gay men to form the Licking County AIDS Task Force, soon to be what there was of the movement in Central Ohio. I saw sadistic Christian cruelty, lonely grief and terrible suffering, and the movement spirit and heroic self-sacrifice of guys who were separated by half a continent from movement epicenters. Secular gay men were a close-up reminder of who Jesus was—"He has borne our griefs and carried our sorrows" and "With his stripes we are healed." I remembered why, as a Fundamentalist, I'd loved him so. The LGBTQ Movement is the most overtly anti-Christian and godless of uprisings. As with Cliff, I reimagined Bible stories in terms of these men, risking life to perform revolting tasks for outcasts. This was Jesus of the Prophetic Bible, Amazing Grace, another conversion.

Prophetic Bible in hand, I had been repeatedly "convicted of Sin" (as we said in evangelistic "crusades") of racism, sexism, militarism and economic elitism, by successive prophetic movements. As it did with the prophetic, the Jesus and other biblical movements, mainstream religion, inspired by the Priestcraft Bible, oppose these redemptive uprisings. What became clear in my research and my life is that these contemporary movements, like those of Scripture, were "of God," transforming History toward the purpose of Creation.

My Secularization course had included Dostoyevsky's Grand Inquisitor. His character famously said religion satisfies a universal need for "miracle, mystery and authority." The Grand Inquisitor exiled Jesus for undermining precisely that, and so with Priestcraft's opposition to everything historically redemptive.

Let's say religion as we know it, paraphrasing Dostoyevsky, satisfies need for meaning (of life), transcendence (otherworldly escape from historical conflict) and community (warmth of closed religious fellowship). Yet Jesus blasphemed Priestcraft's meanings and scriptural base. Likewise Machiavelli's profane political science, Galileo's heretical cosmology, Darwin's violent account of creation, and Marx's damnation of religion as womb of injustice. Secularization reverses focus from transcendence to scientific concentration on the nuts and bolts of the world—disruptive of community, confrontational with religion, a threat to Church hegemony of mind. As does revolution. By contrast, those who have, quoting Jesus, "ears to hear" new ideas and revolutionary visions are empowered to transform the world.

I got into Social Movement theory teaching "Radical Politics and Conscience." As uprisings continued to batter me, as a matter of existential survival, I became a student of them, a connoisseur. I found theoretical underpinnings for what was happening, and in time, theological ones, but first were these naked moments when I was involuntarily renovated by whirling worlds of others who were out of my league. Eventually, I would apply the word "God" to the agency at work, and "Grace"; but for years there was no God, and, god knows, no Grace, just aliens en masse, terrifying whirlwinds of History. My first encounter with each one was shock, shame, and eruption of repressed emotional matter. And that wasn't all. There opened new, hitherto undreamt potentials and redemptive resources. Something was happening, something spiritual, in these explosions of mass humanity.

However violent, these subversive movements had for their

participants a soul. I began visiting the world's insurrections—for their souls. In '88 Saboi Jum of the uprising Kachins in Myanmar sent me to Brang Sang, Baptist school headmaster, their guerrilla leader. I met Brang in a Bangkok hotel way too early after a twenty-four-hour trip. He introduced me to the cell phone, precursor to social media that in two decades would enable revolutions. (My first internet had been Gus Parajon's, reading the Managua newspaper in my home.) Brang's phone was a boxy contraption. He typed its keys, spoke Kachin to someone, and gave it to me. It was Saboi! In Iowa! With Brang was a student from the Burman ruling elite, a true-believer movement convert, sunken cheeks and sockets etched by warfare and privation, lips and busy tongue inadequate to the ideas erupting in the cauldron of his passion.

I mentioned Brang in a Tokyo sermon, and another Burman student, flashing eyes, breathy eloquence, rushed up. "You met Brang Sang?"—touching me, as if Spirit could current up his fingers. I've had that response from black students when I told them of meeting Dr. King, and of all-night drinking bouts with Ralph Abernathy, and from two thousand students reaching for Angela Davis when I introduced her at Vassar. Something was happening: Grace. Not a God-thing. Grace without God.

In Seoul with Peter I met students demonstrating for contact with North Koreans, the single most charismatic event I have witnessed. Yang Sei University paths were chalked with bulletins from the struggle, dorms draped in inflammatory art. The student center was a revolutionary art gallery, hallways crowded with pallets for tear gas victims, those beaten by police truncheons, and others wounded. Students pummeled us with tumbling ideas, movement jargon foreign even in our language. Then, another police attack, and everyone into the street. Peter, who's seen enough of a father's indiscretions, had warned me not to get involved, but the moment overwhelmed him. My image is of Peter, mid-street, rocks sailing, photographing a cop in riot gear chasing a student. Something was happening. Tear-gassed Grace. Nothing about God.

I treasure a rapid-fire succession of images from Peristroika, the spontaneous movements unravelling Soviet Communism. I went to a Moscow suburb to see a dissident just out of the Gulag. On the subway I radiated too-reckless excitement for my companions' caution. "Shut up, George, you'll land us in prison." The dissident lived on floor eighteen in a forest of concrete high rises. We hiked up, not risking the rickety elevator. His tiny flat, walls crammed floor to ceiling with books, was home to an Orthodox underground church where true believers crowded daily for priest-less communion. I asked how Orthodoxy inspired the movement. With familiar darting eyes and unintelligible breathy answers he gave me a mimeographed manifesto being distributed—a Pentecostal babel of jargon and literary excess I got translated back home. Something was happening.

I visited the Solidarity Movement at its summit, Warsaw aflame with movement spirit despite a Soviet crackdown. Solidarity's Information Minister, Januscz Onysczkeiwicz, taught Math at Warsaw University. The campus was radiant with subversive joy like Student hotbeds everywhere, the Math Department a beehive abuzz with recent victories. He wasn't there. A secretary called, said to go to his home. His door was flanked by bruising union guys who frisked and admitted me. Onysczkeiwicz regaled me with uprising stories. "See the Cathedral," he said. Cardinal Wyszinski, Solidarity's patron saint, had built 1500 churches in defiance of the atheist state from there. His disciple, Karol Jozef Wojtyla, borne by movement power, became John Paul II, first non-Italian pope in 500 years. I saw it. Its walls and narrow yard was a bonfire of flagrantly subversive Solidarity regalia forcibly banned elsewhere, as if every movement banner in Poland were unfurled there. No official dared trespass this vortex of Spirit or remove its banners. Something was happening, soon to re-order the world. Grace—with a hint of God.

Sixteen months later, Nov 9, 1989, wearing my professional-holy-man hat, I preached at a Baptist convention in Washington, DC. My title was Frost's "Something there is that does not love a wall," meaning cussed Baptist "walls" I didn't love. Afterward, I visited my nephew John Wagster on Capitol Hill. On his TV was the fall of the Berlin Wall! Berliners were dancing on it, destroying it chip by chip, the supreme movement moment of the late twentieth century—begun, ironically, the very moment of my "wall" sermon. Of course I hadn't meant that wall, but scheduled to preach the next day, I rewrote my sermon and did mean that wall. Ironically, when the Wall went up, August 12, 1961, I was in Norway, and hastened there to see it, and in '89 had just been there again, to see the earthquaking hope behind it. Something was happening that historic night. Grace. The preacher in me found God in it.

For the final lecture in Radical Politics I played the closing movement of Beethoven's Ninth. Its chorus sets to sublime music Schiller's poem "An die Freud" (On Joy), a romantic excess of sentiment about the divine spark in revolutionary human unity. The poem was written in the wake of the American Revolution and on the eve of the French, to be set to music by an unprecedented number of composers over the succeeding quarter-century. I did a voiceover, rising above Beethoven, recalling revolutionary moments from modern history, their leaders' inspiring words, and the ecstatic voices of the uprising peoples. As the chorus rises toward its climax, I played on a separate device the climax of King's "I have a Dream," his elevating rendition of the old Negro Spiritual about the afterlife, nearly but not quite drowned out by the Washington crowd's ecstatic explosion of human unity. "Free at last! Free at last! Thankgodalmighty, I'm free at last!"

THE BREAKTHROUGH OF GOD

I'd suffered disenchantment, but in current social uprisings I'd experienced what anthropologist Anthony Wallace termed "Revitalization Movements," found, among other places, at the beginning of all religions. It was also called Sacralization, transformation of the profane into sacred reality. Compatible with, but over and above mere Sacralization, was biblical testimony in the Prophetic, Jesus and other biblical movements, and of God's presence in such events. "Breakthrough" came to mind, as in onrushing currents opening mounting logjams, moments of redemptive History when God is said by the Bible to be in it. Thus the term, "BREAKTHROUGH OF GOD," a new theme for the latter part of my life. The Religious Bible motivates Religious Evil. But there are texts from the Breakthrough of God, the Prophetic Bible, which move people to redemptive, often heroic action, some of the best things ever done.

My research on the Two Bibles was propelled by the LGBTQ Movement, which was being bitterly opposed by the wider church. One thing became immediately clear: the Prophetic Bible is primarily a function of social movements in biblical times, and is inspiration for such movements in modern times.

The Exodus Movement of slaves from Egypt is archetypal for both Bibles. The Priestcraft Bible sets it as the rescue of God's chosen racial family and beginning of Priestcraft religion. For the Prophets, the God-inspired rebellion was explicitly of Egyptian slaves. To the religion the Prophets said, "Remember, you were slaves in Egypt," rescued as such by God, whose Exodus announcement was "I have heard the cry of my people (the enslaved) and have come down to rescue them." For Priestcraft, the Exodus was proof of the religion's chosenness over and against "the goiim" (the "nations", in other words, the "enemies" of God). For the Prophetic, it is evidence that God's purpose is to rescue the poor and oppressed by empowering and inhabiting their rebellion.

The eighth-century Prophetic Movement was a similar movement led by Prophets, YHWH's spokesmen. When they said, "Thus says YHWH," they spoke in the voice of uprising people impoverished and oppressed by YHWH religion.

The Jesus Movement was more turbulent, exciting and disruptive, gathering "the Kingdom of God," a social movement "from the foundation of the world." "Good news to the poor, release to the captives, empowerment to the oppressed," said Jesus, quoting the Prophets, imitating the Exodus.

The Ekklesia Movement, recorded in the Book of Acts, signifies for the prophetic remnant the Jesus Movement after Jesus' death, a transformed community in and out of jail, "all things in common" (what the Marxists called "original communism"). For Priestcraft, it is the beginning of Christian Religion.

In every case, according to both Bibles, the Prophetic Movements were opposed, often violently, by the practitioners of Priestcraft.

Figuring this out began with my experience of social movements which I saw mirrored in the Exodus of the enslaved from Egypt, Prophetic uprising of the poor and oppressed, Return of Exiles from Babylon, and Jesus and the movement recorded in Acts. Like me, the Great Ones had been inspired precisely by them. The rest of the Bible is about Religion. People who hurl Scripture against the Great Ones, even against the likes of me, quote Religion passages. Applying the theory of the Religious Function in social psychology, it is clear why. It is the religious function to foster community and meaning for life, but uprisings divide community and erupt with blasphemous meanings. In an uprising, it becomes the religious function to oppose it, restore community, and defend established truths. Religious defenders of social stability and traditional meanings find motive and guidance in biblical religion, and in biblical characters who oppose uprisings.

Here's the kicker. If a social uprising embodies the power and presence of God—The Breakthrough of God—it is the ironic social function of religion to oppose that. Biblical priests oppose uprisings led by prophets, Jesus, and the Ecclesia of Acts. Their priestly writings compose most of the Bible. Priestly passages inspire and legitimate religious opposition to the Breakthrough of God in every generation. Therefore, it is the religious function and the biblical mandate to religion always to resist the Breakthrough of God.

Not that biblical Religion opposes the Breakthrough of God as such. It rather interprets God by past breakthroughs. The new one, coming from outside sacred community, generating blasphemous meanings, doesn't look like God. The Civil Rights Movement was passionately resisted by my religion. By the time of the LGBTQ Uprising, religious amnesia had set in. The earlier Movement's symbols and rituals had been gathered into sacred memory, added to gathering avalanches of Grace. The LGBTQ Uprising's drag queens, overt sexuality, anti-Christian rhetoric, official church condemnation, public violations of homophobic biblical passages, and rending in the fabric of Church didn't look like God. For a time at least, most heroes of the Civil Rights Movement opposed the LGBTQ Movement Breakthrough of God, specifically because of how God looked to them, and how that God was not in the new movement.

I find the Bible essentially Prophetic, despite the fact that biblical priests opposed the prophets and most of the Bible is priestly. The Prophetic in Scripture bears witness to the Breakthrough of God, and the Priestly in Scripture opposes it. So, the Bible is the Sacred History of the Breakthrough of God in its paradigmatic classic moments and of religious opposition to it. Passages about breakthrough moments help us interpret the Breakthrough of God when it occurs in our own time. Passages about religious opposition to it forewarn what our religion will inevitably do in reaction: prepare us to be reformed in our religion by the Breakthrough of God.

I was propelled into this study of Religious Evil and the Breakthrough of God by my encounter with the biblical base for the Crusades.

Upended by History

History's not all it's cracked up to be. Agincort, Waterloo, and D-Day are not grand dramas, hinges in time, as if such things exist. They were sweaty grunts, scared beyond their wits, fighting blindly in the dirt, dying dead or living wounded to tell it. The Declaration of Independence was by politicians, some sleazy as Tammany Hall, some demagogic as McCarthy. Deals were made, people bought off. A young lawyer who couldn't possibly have felt up to it, no idea how smart he was, dragged from memory a few dozen phrases and epithets, doing the best he could.

Current History's not Gay Rights realized, redirecting time. It's a few gays, terrified, depressed, fewer recovering homophobes, confused by events on the periphery of life, getting their backs up at more or less the same time, on more or less the same side. That's History. I was there.

It's been a shock of unexpected ordeals, snatching me up, devouring existing values and commitments, hurling me upended into the roaring front end of rushing currents: Carolina streets, a New York college chapel, Central American jungles, Prague Cathedral's yard, a Bangkok hotel room, Yang Sei student center. But nowhere so furious and fateful as a tiny Midwestern town half a continent from where History was being made, a motley collection of ordinary people scantly aware of the LGBTQ Uprising. Most of us sucked into it were straight, initially more or less homophobic, eventually more or less in recovery. LGBTQ people spanned a spectrum: suicidal at the short end, alienated and resigned at the other. Over a half-decade we were at points more awash in History breaking through the homophobic logjam than daily life. It was a new world dawning. Its fabric is a tapestry of stories. Characters are masked to protect the guilty—which we all were. But the stories: they're the God's truth.

The movement in which I'm most notorious, widely reviled and, among a few, most gratifyingly appreciated, is this one.

Treasured friendships came from it. I plunged into its vortex, said "God loves sex" on national TV, and was engulfed in its turbulence almost every day. From its fringe, my denomination designated me its Darth Vader, expelled me and my church, then quite publicly reinstated us. I wasn't black in the Black Movement, female in the Women's, or a student in the Student's. Nor was I Gay. I might as well have been. Enemies announced I was—which I, of course, wasn't about to deny.

The movement, without leadership or positive media coverage, in "faces of the enemy" images I once swallowed whole, facing bitterness, especially from the Church, erupted spontaneously in isolated, disconnected cells. It got tactics from the Civil Rights Movement, most of whose leaders opposed it. Lesbians got inspiration from the Women's Movement, though feminists initially denied the link. Its ritual spirituality consisted of an explosion of liberated sexual promiscuity and flamboyance—a tsunami of horrified shock. I too had been shocked.

Despite enormous advances in the last few years, consensual gay sex was criminal until *Lawrence v. Texas* in 2003, still is in much of the world, still in places a capital offense. Gay people still don't routinely get ordinary rights in employment, taxation, housing rights or police protection, and in many states still can't adopt. Churches still damn them to Hell. The Movement, which swept me up, transformed and revitalized me, is at this writing four decades old, as old as Gandhi's Satyagraha Movement. Because of it, legalized homophobia, while still with us, appears to be in its death throes.

More than other movements, uprising gays enflamed the Religious Right, who with militancy seized homophobic politics as a Crusade. Early on, ex-Student radical Harvey Milk came out and mounted a charismatic bid for San Francisco Council, and for a moment Gay people had a leader. But he was assassinated. Now leaderless, men of studded leather, gay-bar hilarity and bathhouse anonymous sex became, nonetheless, a Movement. Then it suffered the most disastrous calamity—Acquired Immune

Deficiency Syndrome. Men died horrible deaths, decimating whole communities. The Religious Right, with piously veiled glee, proclaimed AIDS to be God's punishment for "sodomy," the favored biblical term, "Abomination," the next favored. President Reagan, beholden to them, let the pandemic rage without intervention. Hospitals rejected patients. Christian families abandoned dying sons, thwarting lovers from visits with legal sanction. The Movement transformed itself to massive disaster relief, heroic care for the dying. Tens of thousands, without religion or medical training, risked lives to offer care that hospitals and churches indignantly refused.

A decade later in the miracles of History, Patrick Swift, a San Francisco oncologist and my son-in-law, like a handful of his colleagues attended malignancies all week, funerals of patients and friends on weekends. As a generation died, they got their spiritual symbol, the AIDS Quilt. Assembled in the Castro, displayed everywhere, it was tiny squares created by loved ones, stitched together into a fifty-four-ton portable cemetery for ninety thousand of the dead.

History for me began with the church youth group. "A child," Isaiah said of the Breakthrough of God, "shall lead." They wanted an LGBTQ speaker. A homophobic youth leader objected, another supported them before the church board, introducing "the homosexuality issue." For a spectrum of reasons the board went with the kids. The leader quit the church, a dreaded result.

Doug Donley, a popular straight kid with gay classmates and movement commitments graduated seminary and wanted ordination. To the ordination committee he voiced "interest in social issues." They asked which ones, and he naively ended his list with "...and...homophobia." In apocalyptic cataclysm, religious homophobia denied him ordination. The church, caught between love for him and unexamined homophobia, went with the love and got him irregularly ordained, thereby breaking ranks on the Christian homophobic solid front. Doug, wrenchingly shorn of naïveté, went on to a distinguished pastoral career.

There rumbled down from the ABC a new dogma: "Homosexual practice is incompatible with Christian teaching." Most denominations have systems of doctrine including one to this effect. Baptists have no doctrine but the Bible. This one was now the whole catechism! Our church classes read gay-affirming theology and sent letters in opposition to the new heresy. To their delight ABC rejected it by a single vote. A year later, though, facing economic reprisals from homophobic churches, the denomination reversed itself. We non-doctrinal Baptists now had a doctrine — still do. We were, still are dogmatically homophobic, our outpost church demoted to heretic.

Bill Keucher, a new church member and retired ABC president I mentioned earlier, would play an unlikely role in the coming ordeal. Bill was a passionate partisan for "Baptist principles" of "soul freedom" and "local church autonomy," individuals and congregations having the right to read and follow Scripture according to their own lights. Theologically moderate, conservative in inclination, no previous experience with LGBTQ people, he was mightily offended at this attempt to dictate doctrine. He would be slow to affirm things LBGTQ and continued to see things in "Baptist principles" terms, but with impeccable reputation and enormous appeal, over a decade of evolving theology, growing affirmation of LGBTQ people he met at church and radical religious freedom, he was our most powerful voice. His actual statements, though, often made us cringe.

A young professor and social justice and academic freedom advocate would become a church leader. Her children had our longest, most honored lineage: grandparents and great grandparents reared and married in the church, and a great-grandfather, called to testify in the Scopes trial for evolution, later a stalwart against McCarthy, our hagiography's chief saint. Women's circles had been named for their missionary great aunts. Their mother, her pedigree and values, would present the Welcoming and Affirming proposal for the vote. A Liberation Theologian with gay friends, who pushed solidarity with the oppressed but was guardian of finances, regularly calculated negative financial impacts of this solidarity. His analysis, pushed by liberation, restrained by concern for wider mission, would complicate each stage. His wife was the town's most socially prominent hostess. She was also in the Feminist Class, which instinctively identified with LGBTQ people, and in the end gave the largest number of "yes" votes. She invited Stan Wolfe, her "apparently gay" hairdresser to church. Fatefully for unfolding developments, he came.

The flamboyant, seat-of-the-pants senior pastor was me. I'd been there seven years when we engaged History, sixteen by the end. I'd been in the LGBTQ Movement at Vassar and had published and preached on the issue. My best friend had come out, as did my son, Peter. My reaction to Peter was negative and positive confusion. Positive, which came to predominate, had to do with confidences he shared with us, a gift. However much Peter might have known about our involvements at gay-friendly Vassar, I was now a Baptist preacher in Midwest homophobia, mostly removed from the issue, except the AIDS Task Force.

I can't imagine the courage it required, but his coming out to us occasioned a dramatic, gratifying maturation. For half a decade he'd been withdrawn, with more than usual hostility and depression, owing mostly to the closet. Suddenly he evidenced a new signature self-confidence and comfort in his own skin. And he began confiding in us. It wasn't all positive, the noisy ugliness of homophobia all around. The gay scene of those days seemed bleak. I feared his life in it might be vastly diminished, even at risk.

As for my homophobia, recovery isn't cure. His coming out evoked my remaining demons, shocking me and adding shame to the mix. Until securely in his confidence, there was a specter of a potential gulf between us. I had a residue of discomfort regarding the details of his sexuality. Until then I hadn't imagined his even having one. Now, it seemed exaggerated. Dan and Chris, contemptuous of homophobia, rejoiced in this cool new facet of their brother, becoming outspoken advocates. Peter himself became outspoken at college. Carol, quiet, constitutionally modest, careful, and very thoughtful (my polar opposite) would ultimately evidence an emotional support for LGBTQ people that would be simply unanswerable.

Two families got the church into Columbus' Gay Pride Parade, the first church ever to participate. Three dozen straight people left from worship with a banner proclaiming the church's support—like blacks marching forth from Movement churches. Most had their first encounter with bike dykes, drag queens and public affection, taking it in good-humored discomfort, then had the uncanny experience of being flamboyantly cheered for two hours by ten thousand along the route. A church, a Baptist church, in their parade! We were swept up in movement charisma—the breath of History. Most of us had a first taste of religious homophobia. Truly hateful people lined the route, many identifying Baptist, waving Bibles, invoking a sadistic, homophobic deity. All our folks were changed, got a vision of History happening, a ministry needed. TV coverage was of drag queens, hatemongers, and the Baptist Church. We had a public identity.

Matt, a college dropout, came out to me. I offered him opportunity for testimony in worship. So this privileged, moderate church heard the terrifying story of the closet, its dreadful toll, crushing humiliation, malignant loneliness, vortex of self-hatred, sucking quicksand of insanity, and suicide attempts. Matt had a sweet humility. His innocence gave even stupid condescending questions honest answer. You began to hear this curious theme in the homophobic undertone: "I don't like homosexuals. But Matt's all right."

Then Stan, the hairdresser, suffering homophobia against himself. Then Barry, a homeless bard living on the bike path. He'd come out in his teens. Accepting his church's damnation, he'd suffered ex-gay ministries abuse, went to Oral Roberts U. for a miracle from The Man himself, and finally succumbed to self-abuse of the damned. He became our showcase ex-ex-gay. Now it was, "I don't like ... except Barry, Matt and Stan." By the time

History was done with us, Stan was hairdresser to us all. Matt was in seminary. Barry ran his music business in our building, his "gay contemporary Christian music" a bit of a stretch for our classicists. We offered Thanksgiving dinner for "people not welcome at home," then Christmas dinner, then, at an attendee's request, a Valentine's dance—all advertised in the newspaper. Baptist churches went apoplectic over the dance. Rumors ricocheted of demonic sexual delights in the baptistry. In fact, those at the dance were shy as middle schoolers. Hardly anybody danced, maybe none, but when they left, their heads were held high.

This run of crunchy stories might imply a gathering momentum. Not at all! A current of straightism and homophobia ran deep. The town was elitist, Republican, far from the madding crowd. The church, suffering a steady stream of defections for stands on a scattershot of issues, was weak, attendance down, finances fragile, wounds fresh. A senior couple whose kin had abandoned ship in a pique were the most wounded. When we finally voted to embrace History, they resigned with a fiery letter.

The most open, unselfconscious opponent was a septuagenarian, lifelong member with a long Baptist resume. She attended all discussions and spoke clearly in generosity of spirit against our emerging gay-friendliness. Matt especially enjoyed sparring with her, even enjoyed a guided tour through the nuts and bolts of her heterosexism. She voted NO at every juncture, and said why, but when a lesbian couple had their wedding at church, she invited them over and with self-deprecating humor laughed about her biblical prudery. A friend came out to her, revealed his HIV and suicidal intentions. She took him in, flushed his pills, restored his integrity and saved his life.

For weeks the church newsletter ran articles pro and con. Despite a substantial number opposed, perhaps even a majority, only one was willing to write in opposition. Others complained that the series was a setup. Those in support could write sparkling, intellectual essays. Those against weren't talented writers and had to borrow quotes from homophobic publications. The one who wrote against, a fortyish high school grad, was uncomfortable writing. Everyone knew that, and expressed appreciation.

A hothead liberal defender of losing causes shocked us with vitriolic homophobic potshots, bigotry transcending—or subscending—ideology. He confided that he'd had a youthful incident of homosexual abuse acknowledging its tangle in his attitudes. Still, he resigned with a bitter open letter, quoting hair-raising scriptures, quoting his daughter, asking, "Do we go to a gay church now?" Later, he was referred to a lesbian physician who was a new church member. They became friends and talked about the issue. He eventually wrote a letter regretting the damage he had likely done, asking forgiveness and re-admittance. It did more good than perhaps any document of the decade.

Outreach expanded: potlucks, dances, marches. Our reputation mushroomed through pastoral counseling, discussion, and support groups at the county's one gay bar. An LGBTQ Sunday School class worked through religious traumas of the closet and revisionist scholarship on the six "texts of terror" hurled at them from Scripture. Three years passed, only the three gay men were members and only rarely did we have a gay or lesbian visitor. By now this was clear: LGBTQ people were so wounded by preachers and religious institutions that most couldn't imagine wanting a church ever again. They repeatedly said so.

Debate whether to formally become Welcoming and Affirming centered on two concerns, neither one "the issue" itself. Most thought our LGBTQ ministries were "Christlike," someone said, everyone at least welcoming of the three gay men. Scariest of the surviving concerns were "cost," and given that, "What's the point?" The latter was pressed by the church liberal most active in Democratic politics, that there seemed no payoff for the church's unique radical mission. She said, "They couldn't care less, and won't come to this or any church whatever we do." No one had answers, except "but it's the right thing to do."

As for cost, there was no calculating it—except one thing. Our equivalent of the bishop was a member, as were his predecessors.

Homophobia was too deep to tolerate a Welcoming and Affirming Ohio Baptist executive. His wife was a bright diamond of a member. Their loss would be high profile nationwide, denying a prize facet of our face. This beloved couple, our special charge, would suffer impossible alternatives and be deeply hurt. At the vote, most "NO's" were in their behalf.

They resigned that day. It didn't help, though. The homophobic apocalypse was so terrifying that he soon resigned his job anyway. Ironically, the church they chose after moving to another state was Welcoming and Affirming.

Seven years after the youth group debate, six after Doug's rump ordination, five after the Gay-Pride Parade, four after Matt came out in church, three after opposing doctrinal homophobia, two after the Valentine Dance, one after the "issue" was officially brought, after five months of Baptist process, we voted. All discussions included Barry, Matt or Stan, straights and gays talking to each other. The vote was two to one, to join the "Association of Welcoming and Affirming Baptists" which some of us had helped to form. Five members left. The other "NO's" accepted the majority decision. That was it. It was over. We moved on.

Brother Jed was a local religious kook and nationally notorious street preacher. He espoused apocalyptic theology and "confrontational evangelism," terrifying into repentance the vulnerable in street crowds. He and scruffy disciples came to our sidewalk toting signs: "God hates fags;""Anal intercourse lessons;" "Church of Sodom." We invited them in, but "God wants us on the sidewalk." They visited often, making obscene chants, as did Fred Phelps and his group from Westboro Baptist, Topeka, Kansas, the country's most outrageous Christian homophobes. Their T-shirts read "Repent or Perish." We made our own T-shirts, "Welcoming and Affirming" on the front, and on the back, "REPAINT OUR PARISH."

I received a visit from a colleague I didn't know. He opened with a laundry list of off-the-record disclaimers. He would not own up to this meeting if accused, and was there "solely from conscience," to snitch. He snitched that Baptists were secretly meeting to remove us from the local association—of which, a century past, we'd been a founding member. I first heard the oxymoron "disfellowship." Snitch made, the conscientious Baptist left.

Baptists became possessed with demonic homophobia in response to History's invasion through our church. Bland conservative preachers averse to conflict became passionate and public in denunciation of what they boasted ignorance of except for six phrases of the Bible's 31,103 verses. Red of face, carotid arteries pulsing, voices straining, they broadcast vindictive apocalyptic warnings and propaganda from homophobic cesspools. They changed the association constitution in an irregular vote, elevating religious homophobia above key ideals of Baptist tradition.

The association president issued a news release about us—a tactical miscalculation. Having stirred controversy for a decade on a range of issues, we were media savvy. Our computer stored address labels to media outlets, and we knew how to write for journalists. We recorded the homophobic blather of our opponents and quoted both sides, replacing the association's pious euphemisms with the actual hateful words of our attackers. They refused comment to reporters who went with quotes we provided, exposing Christian homophobia at its worst—the goal of nonviolent resistance. This would shape the final outcome years later. It also inspired feature stories. Every journalist, except those who were part of the Christian media, identified as gay or gay-friendly. Most stories were from our point of view. What the homophobes were saying got covered from a gay point of view. The media became a medium for evangelism. Only once did flamboyant me let down my guard.

An ABC Evening News reporter did a story on us. The crew engulfed the town, setting up lights and miles of cable. Food service and dressing room trucks lining the street. She interviewed me, talking off the cuff, off topic, for an hour or so, loosening me up, before getting into it. At one point, seeming personally perturbed, she asked me, confidentially, how I responded to those who said gay sex was damned. I laughed. Describing God as the Creator who "loved" the Creation and is also the Creator of sex, I quipped that "God loves sex." Overwhelmed with a feeling of heroism, I then said that if God didn't love my lesbian and gay parishioners, I would choose to be damned with them. I hoped like hell she'd include that brave line. Two nights later, tuning in to watch myself on national TV, the program opened with my interviewer showing "a gay-friendly Ohio pastor" saying, "God loves sex." I still get ribbed.

An artist, with prophetic tongue spouting like Amos at manifold hypocrisies beneath our elitism, was good for us in ways we needed, but schizophrenic. Many went out of their way to rescue her, taking her into their homes. She abandoned meds, fatally disrupted her class, launched an Amos-like attack in earshot of worship and full view of traumatized children. Fragile lesbians thought it Brother Jed on the rampage. Skilled women walked her to a park and talked her down for hours. We offered to pay for psychiatric help. When she refused and persisted in pathology, we made the unbearable decision to have police prohibit her from the premises. Next Sunday our psychological professionals stood guard in case she should come. Ironically, Matt preached his first sermon that day, opening his ministry to the de-churched.

A radio journalist asked, "What do you tell the children?" I offered to round up some so she could "ask them." Mark and Lucy thought it "cool!" to be on radio, and biked right over. Their answers, broadcast statewide, were sophisticated and direct. Years later at the church celebration of their high school graduation, a tape of the interview was played. New LGBTQ members hearing it fresh were in tears. Their best answer was to "What do your friends think?" They laughed together. Lucy said, "Oh, they think we're weird. But they don't know any gays yet. They will. They'll get over it." Beginning with Mark and Lucy, this little midwestern church produced a generation of kids altogether without homophobia.

With ironic help from the press, we spread a Welcoming and Affirming gospel worldwide. We got letters from across the US,

Europe, Australia and New Zealand, stories of the closet, traumas of Christian bigotry, gratitude—to us, who'd done not a blessed thing. Early letters went in the newsletter, but eventually there were too many. Someone made a loose-leaf Book of Letters. It grew to hundreds of pages, a sacred anthology of pain, heroism and pure joy. It held honored place on the communion table. You'd see people leafing through, copying words—like rubbings in medieval cathedrals. But for a brass cross on the table, the Book of Letters was this free church, low church, Baptist church's only icon.

And so, thirteen months after the vote, ten after the snitch, nine after official contact, after four irregular meetings where we were libeled and condemned without evidence or rebuttal, our local Baptist Association voted to disfellowship their lone Welcoming and Affirming church. The meeting was carnival-like, a song leader rousing them with a hymn sing of praise songs as votes were counted, recalling the mob spirit at witch burnings and lynchings. Afterward, our delegation stood in the street outside, held lighted candles, and sang "Amazing Grace."

Feelings? There was the sense of having borne the faithful witness, and kept to patient endurance, as exhorted in Scripture, but mostly we felt depression and guilt. This historic church was officially alienated from its association family. However right we may have felt on the issues, having heard so many criticisms for so long, so many accounts of damage done, we couldn't escape the dread that where there is so much sulfuric smoke there must be at least some hellacious fire. At any rate, it was over. At last, on to other things.

A Baptist LGBTQ Movement

The next Sunday a fragile lesbian couple sat on a back row. History, by no means done with us, was back. After that there was hardly a Sunday unmarked by such visits. We'd recognize their visage of terror, a glance at the ceiling as for lightning strikes, their huddling in the back as against attack, and their bolt for the door at the end. We devised a strategy to head them off, give proper hug, make introduction, get addresses. Many returned, recognizable by a fresh look of empowerment. "We've read about you," they'd say. Some were those who'd sworn off churches. I had the chutzpa to ask why they'd come to a church after all. "CHURCH?" a rough lesbian barked. "This ain't church! You're thrown out of church like us." Despised and rejected ... borne our griefs ... carried our sorrows.

A Catholic nun came, known in the lesbian underground as a safe sister who'd had it with the closet, resigned her order, and come out with the Baptists. Also a defrocked pastor who'd come out and lost his family, asking, "Will you take me too?" From these articulate ecclesiastical casualties we heard all we could bear about the dark underbelly of Christian triumphalism. But that isn't the half of it. The man would be an inspiring leader, calling us to something unimagined. The nun would be reinstated by her bishop, sent to another state and glorious ministry, sending a pack of letters, irreverently funny and authentic stories of real ministry among real people. If there's ever a new scripture, her "Epistles to the Granville church" will be included. The Breakthrough of God.

There was a gay couple of fourteen years, both preacher's daughters. They came early, joined the choir and were quickly beloved. They had rough days in their relationship, something we worried about. One Sunday, one gave her testimony, then called the other up, and placed a ring on her finger—they hadn't had rings—and pledged renewal of lifelong love before a spellbound congregation.

A newcomer joined, Southern Baptist, shy, a professor with exceptional credentials. She'd never had a date. She became a church officer, an articulate theological giant—incredible to see. And a physician with a conservative past, a brash mover-shaker and controversial button-pusher. She was regular and conspicuous, but resisted membership. "Not a joiner," she said. "I'm a loner, couldn't belong to a church with clients." She didn't trust community. "Give it a try," I nudged.

She did, got embraced, dropped her guard and exploded with affection. "I was bifurcated," she said in her jargon, "Jesus here, love-life there. Now I'm just me, one." It was a nuclear fusion with earth-moving energy release. She was closeted at work, out on the scene and now at church. She refused an interview for the paper, got the guilts, came out at work and instantly became a public force for LGBTQ empowerment. I asked her for a lecture on healing. "I'm no healer, just a pill pusher." "But you empower people." "Oh," she said, "that." So she presented a profound secular expression of ministry. Far from avoiding clients at church, she began sending, then bringing them, saying there was something going on they needed to see. It was she who gave us a name. "Evangelism"—which made secular liberals, who thought that was something fundamentalists did, uncomfortable. But she'd been converted by these liberals—Evangelism.

There wasn't conflict over issues most churches fought over: LGBTQ people teaching Sunday School, holding office, or the big two: ordinations and weddings. At the first wedding request there wasn't a ripple. An out-of-town couple asked me. I got the church's okay, counseled them, married them, felt we were on the front end of History's wave and wrote it up in the newsletter. The first for a church couple was a chapel wedding, attendants, reception, the works, truly joyous, done by the church. We said, "In trust for the state until the state should catch up." Through the nineties, we did more gay than straight weddings.

A staff member came out to me, then to friends, and one by one, to the congregation. She and her husband divorced. She had another job, too, so like others was out only at church. Straight people needed educating about closet realities like secret-keeping and awful consequences. We ran newsletter lessons. Unintentionally, I violated the rules with a phrase in a Christmas letter inadvertently outing her. Happily it was caught before mailing. Unhappily, it's my practice to handwrite personal notes. I'd spent weeks penning them. It was too late to do them over. Somebody donated white-out. I whited out two words on 600 letters—an all-night reality ritual in the brave new world.

On a summer Sunday, the rag-tag summer congregation in ratty leisure attire, Adrianne came, off-the-shoulder party dress, heels, stockings, flowing hair, masculine features. I confess to thinking "Please God, not this too." I greeted ... her ... him ... with no background for this. A new lesbian came to church, and I noticed that Adrianne had chosen to sit next to her. She blurted, "He ... she ... What do you say? Sat next to me! I remembered we always hug passing the peace, thought of nothing else until the dread hugging time, then quickly grabbed Adrianne, said 'Peace-of-God,' and sunk into waves of guilt. I, who'd finally found where I could be my oddball self and get hugs, stoved up giving them to another." My pastoral comfort: "You weren't the only one."

Adrianne came back, dressed again to the nines. "I've read of you for a year, meaning to come, but chickening out, expecting one more rejection." At last, she came. "The woman next to me," she said, visibly moved, "hugged me! Warmest I ever got! I'm home!" Again turned upside down, I had much to learn, to flush. But she was a healer, steeped in Native American shaman spirituality. The next summer an upscale neighboring church shared services with us while its sanctuary was under renovation. A family of theirs emerged from their SUV, coats and ties, dresses, squeaky clean. Adrianne handed them bulletins at the door in T-shirt and tight red shorts. They didn't notice! She took me to a Chrystal Club national convention, her family of choice, to give the keynote. I, a recovering Southern Baptist homophobe, orated to 300 six-foot women with Adam's apples on the Good Samaritan—"The Good Transgender."

Approaching the microphone it struck me, my improbable journey to this convention. I was transported back, not to the Sit-in (that wasn't the beginning), but to the Administration Building terrace at Wake Forest, my first social movement, my first act of civil disobedience: a ballroom step, giving up not-dancing-for-God for God, laying aside the totem that defined and gave me power, beginning the long, tumbling pilgrimage toward this unlikely moment.

There was a Lutheran pastor, out to and ministering with gay people, referring them to us. She had been outed to her Bishop. He fired her, and said to clean out her office. We voted her in as adjunct pastor for LGBTQ ministries, "T" for Adrianne, "Q" the rest of us. When she went to empty her office her files were in boxes outside. That night there was a storm. The wrought iron cross atop her church, the town's tallest God-spire, was struck by lightning and toppled, upright head first in the ground. There is a God! She founded an ecumenical glory-days ministry unique in kind, seized the wave loosed by our notoriety, riding it in outreach of unbelievable proportions, an e-mail congregation of 400 mostly closeted, mostly rural people with no outlet for nourishment or open life. She eventually worked herself out of a job. Hers was once the most effective such organization in a dozen counties. Scores of LGBTQ people having come out, it was equipped to reshape a socio-political landscape that no longer needed it.

She brought "de-churched" people, the wounded, phobic of church. Ann suffered a rare disease devouring her legs. We found a doctor who amputated them. She showed off her prostheses, learned to walk without a cane, biked, roller bladed, and gave inspirational demos in church and schools. Ann was a rock star, though one kid fainted when she passed around her leg.

Sue had genetic disorders leaving her unable to stay erect and barely able to speak. She too became a star. Nearly anything can be overcome. A pastor from another denomination did her sabbatical studying our "charismatic oddness." Her first Sunday, she and her husband were ushered by Adrianne, sat next to a church dog, across from Sue, and also Ann who laid her prostheses on the pew. The husband was heard whispering, "Dorothy, we're not in Kansas anymore."

Most of its 180 years the church was too homogeneous for authenticity, its last African-Americans dead, conservatives fled, poor and broken, out of reach. But the Breakthrough of God changed everything, our LGBTQ alphabet soup not half of it. They pushed open doors that no one knew were closed. African-Americans who preferred black music and preaching, brother-and-sisterhood, but sick of preacher-homophobia, embraced us honkeys to be welcomed and affirmed. Same for Native Americans, Asians, Hispanics, the poor, disabled folks struggling with steps and heavy doors in a 120 year old building. Then came a couple with three divorces between them, cynics about religion, witches into Wicca, goddess-worshippers. High school dropouts sat with PhD's; Nazarenes, Pentecostals and Holy Rollers suffocated in our uptight worship; Lutherans, Catholics and Episcopalians found it way too loosey-goosey. The issue was diversity, more than we knew how to handle, but we thrived. A researcher wrote a book on our dealing with controversy, called it a remarkable complex of alliances, disagreeing on one thing, bonded on another, no camps or cliques. There were. But it hung together.

Barry, Matt and Stan's class grew, staging for LGBTQ people as they crept back to church; worked through anger, guilt, doubt and Bible, then mostly moved on to another class. For a while it was our most dynamic cadre, a Liberation Theology base community, the oppressed seizing their Gospel back, finding in it and giving out of it miraculous empowerment.

We started a Habitat for Humanity house. A disproportion of our lesbians had construction skills, enough to build a house on our own. It was the Charisma, charging enthusiasm of the moment, raw gratitude. A straight contractor from the old crowd was straw boss. Habitat International required diverse churches and traditions sweating together, but we documented more ecumenicity, way more diversity than all the other churches.

Everybody took a role, but it was the self-labeled "power-tool dykes" who made us hum, flower and laugh.

The house-raising was unforgettable, everybody there, a bare foundation that by dark was a closed-in shell with shingles, windows, and locked doors. Next door forty churches were building, all male workers, women bringing lunch. Most of our workers were women, occasionally all women. Lunches, flowers and 'faaabulous desserts' were by gay men (lots of laughs about that). The boss wrote a love poem to "Women who don't love men" and got plenty of loving—the very week Southern Baptists required its women to be "subservient" to their husbands. Straw boss said he was subservient to a bunch of power-tool dykes for a year, and heartily recommended it. Most weren't good at measuring lumber, etc. We were taught—to measure!—by Dave Martin, a highly skilled blind member. "The blind leading the blind," we said.

A lesbian and a gay couple had a baby. Its dedication featured the kid, four parents, and eight grandparents—a tableau of Grace. Another couple tried to get pregnant, and after failures and a surgery, finally it took. One of the moms had been Catholic and for her family asked if their dedication could include a Catholic baptism, touching, shall we say, all the bases. Why not? We'd done one for a straight ex-Catholic, using the ritual, holy oil, holy water, all of it. I'd asked my Episcopal colleague about holy oil and water. He said, "Vegetable oil and tap water. Boil the hell out of it." In this case, though, I asked a Catholic priest friend if he'd do it. He did, holy oil, water, Latin mumbo-jumbo, the whole nine yards. A third lesbian couple came looking bloomy and radiant: another pregnancy. I meekly suggested maybe lesbians should look into birth control.

The officiant at an ecumenical communion service had worked vigorously against Welcoming and Affirming among Methodists. Lay-server was Matt, by now the most notorious activist in town. The homophobic pastor passed bread and cup to Matt, who then served him. The Body of Christ.

There were complaints. Most heard was, "We're a one-issue church," aimed mostly at me. Accusers were a mixed bunch. Some yearned for neglected missions or themes. Some wanted a spectrum of potentials; others church growth among "regular people." A few had plain old homophobia. One's concern was for visitors who were offended by so much LGBTQ reference, though most visitors were gay.

To the stubborn pastor it seemed issues were plenty diverse. "One-issue" complaints were high during the Habitat project, which then was our "one issue." Feminist spirituality and politics, reproductive freedom, biblical revisionism, denomination reform, and the Baptist Peace Fellowship were our issues. We assisted Denison in a Holocaust Remembrance project. Spiritual renewal and Environmentalism supported new classes. To hardheaded me, LGBTQ meant less an "issue" and more a "kairos," an engulfing encounter with History. We had a particular Calling that, for its all-too-brief time, must be followed wherever it led, like Civil Rights churches, dissident churches of Eastern Europe, Bishop Tutu's churches, and base communities in Latin America.

We pastors found that LGBTQ marriage ceremonies weren't enough. Lasting relationships were much harder to maintain. Absence of family support, social status, healthy role models and no tradition of permanent relationships made maintenance of households a monumental task. Straights who'd known few divorces, when favorite lesbian couples broke up, were offended, disillusioned. Proud for being ahead of History, they'd put these norm-breaking marriages on a pedestal. Picking up pieces took a lot of pastoral time and emotional energy. The pastors, it turned out, me especially, were in over our heads. New structures and new techniques awaited invention.

Matt was our first LGBTQ person in seminary. We had done nine ordinations, eight of women, more than any ABC church of the time. Inability to ordain was the only serious consequence of being disfellowshipped. No Baptists anywhere had ordained an out gay person, so Matt's seminary decision was a matter of taking his considerable frame through the eye of a needle. With God all is possible. We licensed him without a blink, with indeed a standing ovation, both for Matt and no doubt, for the hell of it. Before he graduated we had five gays in seminary and four straights, eight more standing ovations, and the church was back in the ordination business. All indeed is possible.

We made application for remote membership in the Rochester, New York, ABC region. There were mutual visits, a flurry of documents, New Yorkers who admired us for taking the lead. Almost to a person they were swept up in the kairos, the turning back of a demonic spirit, the seizing of the Breakthrough of God. They took us in. By then five other ABC churches had gone Welcoming and Affirming and been disfellowshipped. Four other regions took the others in. Now the Rochester Region has a bunch of non-geographical Welcoming and Affirming churches stretching across the country.

Our dismissal from ABC national was delayed, and a study group studied. We were invited to appeal our dismissal, and to be retained at the national level. Our appeal was written by two angels, as if sent to us in the Breakthrough of God just for this purpose. One was Bill Keucher, who'd written a slew of books on "Baptist Principles," "Soul Freedom" and "local church autonomy." The other was Dave Ball, a true-believer convert to these principles. A Methodist reverend, he'd being sanctioned by his bishop for disobedience. He and his Catholic wife, who wanted to go to seminary and be ordained, had abandoned their heritage and come to us specifically to exercise religious liberty. He was a lawyer who'd been ordained and had a PhD in Theology and Law.

These two exceptional scholar/writers marshaled and documented the evidence, both of irregularities in procedures against us and relevant legal principles from Baptist tradition. These the lawyer crafted into a uniquely readable and persuasive brief. We were first disfellowshipped, so were heard first by the ABC board. Because the brief was unanswerable, we won, though by a single vote, and were reinstated. The homophobic forces called for a lunch recess. They lobbied conservative delegates, who heard the other appeals, most written by their pastors. The board rejected them one by one.

We heard about a lesbian tragedy in a nearby town. Heather Rittenhouse grew up in her church there, where her father was a leader. She did seminary and was ordained by her church. She later came out—to herself and, by the Grace of God, to a woman with whom she fell in love. They became "roommates" and surreptitiously went to LGBTQ events. Her father found out, confronted then outed her, insisting that his daughter's ordination be revoked. I didn't know her, but invited myself over, heard her story and urged her to come with us.

I offered re-ordination, but she was too wounded. She and her partner came to church, sitting in the back. For a year she came, a mangled soul. Eventually she opened up a little, and we spied evidence of her gifts. During conversations with Rochester we offered her a part-time pastoral position, which, surprisingly, she accepted. She blossomed, and grasped the negotiations as a major player, impressing them, not to mention us, with self-confident, articulate presence. When we were admitted they elected her representative to ABC's general board, the first openly gay person in its history. There she found her voice, forceful and prophetic, which she brought to our pulpit and to confrontations with homophobic reality. Now she was ready for re-ordination. We conducted it, an unforgettable service, lasting much of a Sunday afternoon, involving people from across the US It was an ecstatic celebration of the Breakthrough of God in and through the life of this charismatic woman.

One Sunday, a lesbian we'd barely noticed stood at the sharing time. She said she'd snuck in the back pew, and had been accosted by brazen straights who had the nerve to trespass her guarded space "with ... well ... welcome and affirmation." She'd returned, and again, getting the Spirit, moved up row-by-row. Now here she was, halfway to the front, putting into words what had been sensed by many, that her life, like History around her, was changed.

A conservative woman moved to town to be near her daughter, a church member. She meant to find another church. She attended once, twice, then saw "something going on here" and joined, "though there's a lot I don't agree with." She challenged me on theology and biblical interpretation, voting "NO" on whatever issue at whichever meeting. One Sunday she approached and quietly said, "When I came I thought homosexuality a Sin. I don't now... because ... 'By their fruits you shall know them.'"

Lucy, a teen, asked to interview me for a school project "about homophobia." I suggested she interview gay people. "Well, I was going to interview Matt, but he isn't here and time's run out. I don't know who is and who isn't ... and ... well, I can't ask, 'Are you or aren't you?'" As we happened to be next to a lesbian covey clucking together, I swished Lucy into it. They took her to lunch at a nearby greasy spoon. Get this picture: Lucy, the most hormonal heterosexual with-it of small-town teenagers, at a restaurant amid a half-dozen howling lesbians talking dyke-talk, regaling her with stories from the closet, locals agape in nearby booths—The New Jerusalem!

My beloved Carol has been a quiet presence in the exploits here mentioned. She's my fiercest defender, though she's also appalled at about half my shenanigans. Least of anyone I know does she seek or even permit the limelight, exactly the opposite of me, need it be said. But there were three exceptions in this engagement with History which none who were present will forget. All had to do with Peter. At a church board session when squabble dragged on unproductively she began to weep. The din of raised voices silenced as one-by-one noticed. She spoke, choking, but eloquent, of her experience as the mother of a very gay kid. Discussion resolved.

At the association meeting which sanctioned us, the close vote was announced and the moderator declared the meeting adjourned, calling on a saintly old black preacher to lead in prayer. He rose and said, "Dear Lord ..." but my gentle, generous, careful and utterly unpretentious Carol rose, in front of God and everybody, shouting, "NO! I didn't get a ballot, nor did most of us from Granville. The number of votes exceeds the total number of delegates here. Somebody stuffed the ballots." The saintly preacher wilted, the moderator swatted her mallet, adjourned, and left.

Then came Granville's annual four-day, mid-America patriotic Fourth of July celebration. Town council, on religious liberty grounds, had granted Brother Jed's homophobes a permit for their obscene demonstration. We'd schooled our folks to not let themselves be drawn into argument with his provocative vitriol, but to be a silent, dignified presence available for counseling if any listeners seemed upset. Carol and I, walking Oscar (our ninety-pound German Shepherd), caught sight of Brother Jed's inflammatory banners and heard his obnoxious voice. We moved toward him to hear. Vilifying our church with pornographic slander, he saw me and hailed me for "teaching butt-fucking in the baptistry." I smiled, according to plan. Then he declared, "Williamson raised his son to be a butt-fucker." Carol without drawing breath, preceded by Oscar, mounted the steps, thrust her red face into his, and this loveliest of women whom I'd never heard utter profanity in anybody's audition but mine, shouted into his bulging eyes and gaping mouth, "YOU GODDAMNED SONOFABITCH. SHUT YOUR FUCKING MOUTH!" She whirled, dragged off snarling Oscar to a screaming, stomping ovation from the crowd, who then dispersed, having heard it all.

A weekday class of quirky lay Bible scholars took up biblical women. They retold stories from the woman's point of view, finally writing a "Gospel of Mary Magdalene," finding in Mary's imagined spin a name for their experience. Without intending to, they tracked the adventure of their church through her and discovered the "thirty-five 'immediatelies.'" The word "immediately" appears thirty-five times in Mark's highly charged Gospel, nine in rapid-fire through Mark's opening: Jesus off on his mission, "immediately" twisting here, "immediately" turning there, "immediately" rushing from town to town, giving Gospel, as it were, over his shoulder. They discovered what a kairos is, a moment crowded with overlapping time, impossibilities happening and   immediately happening again, everyone confused, most offended, but a remnant handful, for God knows what reason, seizing the kairos and riding it over the flooding waterfall of History. It was they who said the church had encountered a kairos moment in History. With no preparation or any idea at all what they were doing and immediately doing again, we had, "oh, what the hell," seized it. None of us, they said, would ever be the same. Grace!

Grace, before it is anything else, is the crack inherent in the otherwise ironclad, unbreakable laws of nature and history. Grace is the capacity for unchangeable things to change; the charisma, hidden in the depths of historically powerless people, to acquire irresistible power; the long string of benevolent unpredictables that have characterized human History. Grace is the final unrealism of the realisms: the reality, despite all, of the finally open future.

MY CALLING

In the end, what constitutes, what hounds and thrills me, is inescapable suspicion that I suffer a Calling from God. This isn't something I'm proud of or can document. It isn't in any sense a singling-out. It's just there, light from behind, warming my backside, narrowly lighting the way ahead, casting a shadow toward where I'm bound when, occasionally, I'm in it; a nagging distraction in the general dark, when as usual I'm not. It's inherited from Daddy, a Calvinist potato-chip executive who suffered a Calling, then from Great Ones whose unmistakable Calling lights up the world. My suspicion of and struggle with it pretty well sums up my lurching life.

"Calling," I say, "from God"—a complicated confession. Fundamentalists have made me wary of theism. I'm pure atheist regarding their biblical god. The theism of spiritualists and, for the most part mystics leaves me agnostic. It is God as seen in and behind the life of Jesus that I find illuminating, though not finally sufficient. My fragile theism comes from my Calling. I have a Calling therefore I believe. God, as I know God, comes to me only in the hearing and living out of my Calling, as exemplified in the life of Jesus in his Calling.

Beginning with the Civil Rights Movement, my pilgrimage through the serial social movements was illuminated by fateful Cliff-flashbacks. What happened to me reminded me of Bible stories. As if Cliff were right there, I'd rehash the old story and set what was occurring in a biblical context. Holding out for a biblical life, running my life through the stories, told me my name.

Here in eight images is what I think I've been Called to:

IMITATE JESUS

My Calling begins with JESUS. In Cliff's perverse influence, I see him as at least a little like me. I'm a religious dropout who never escaped religion, an intellectual lightweight, who, though eager to learn, am more compelled to action. So was Jesus. His most revered contemporaries led scholarly lives. He didn't. There's no story of his reading a book, going to school, no proof he was even literate—a disciple, it seems, of John the Baptizer, a non-intellectual charismatic activist. He may have been with Essenes by the Dead Sea, but it didn't take. He went with what he knew by age thirty. He was religious in early life, but he grew increasingly critical of religion, and finally abandoned it. He was a non-professional healer and exorcist, a social reformer, but not in any known tradition. He was a teacher, not of facts, concepts, or, significantly, of ideas—of life, the "Way" of life, existence. And God. But not the Law-giver war-God from scripture or the angry God of his beloved Prophets. It was God as he lived with God, God-in-lived-life, "Abba"—a term best translated "Daddy."

Jesus knew a lot, and scholars were impressed. But it's not clear what, or how he came by it. He knew the Creation stories, crystallizing his sense of God's intentions for History and his own intimacy with nature. He knew the Exodus, had original ideas about its significance. The prophetic spin on Exile and Return were formative. He knew the "greatest commandment," to love God and neighbor, that no law should supersede it. He knew other biblical laws, but the ones he quoted he dismissed or explicitly violated, thereby getting in a passel of trouble. It isn't clear if any actually guided his choices, except maybe the Jubilee commandment "to proclaim release to the captives and recovery of sight to the blind." All of this is my Calling. None seems out of reach.

Jesus knew the Prophets best. Did he get disciplined instruction? Who knows? But he knew them as if he'd met them, knew what they were like, what they confronted, their impact. He was popularly recognized as "one of the Prophets." He embodied them, but not exactly. He shared their raging moral judgment, but more gently. He differed in his hope. Theirs was Exile and Return, and that moral failure would lead to Exile, but God assured a morally restored order of True Faith. For him Exile was now, this wicked and adulterous generation, an epithet of the Baptizer. Hope was the Kingdom of God, also now, coming from the foundation of the world, fully present in the Breakthrough of God. Unlike the Prophets, his passion was this current life, lived in Hope for God's surely coming future, animated with Love, structured by Justice, won in Peace: healings, exorcisms, parables, street theater, charismatic traveling community, martyr's death and reports among followers of resurrection. And the Breakthrough of God. All these but martyrdom and resurrection feel like my Calling.

My preaching about Jesus is shaped by social movements and social science. What went on in my head and came out my mouth wasn't God embodied in a pious religious teacher with twelve eager male religious students. It was God invading ordinary time, embodied by a prophetic charismatic leader and cadre of twenty or so men and women. It was God, no icon of religious observance, but of Creation, stirring into Being a more just, more lovingly nourishing social order in the ongoing Creation of History.

In my quirky theology Jesus isn't a once-for-all incarnation of the Wholly Other for the purpose of Salvation. He's charismatic leader of the paradigmatic Breakthrough of God. This is a recurring incarnation, forever upending History, setting it again toward its destiny. Jesus' historical type is not Philosopher, such as Plato, not magician or miracle worker (though he allegedly did some of that), not Statesman or Empire Builder.

He's no author or discoverer of unknown truths. He's not at all like Mohammed, the Buddha, or any Religious Founder. I think of him more like Francis, the young Luther, Gandhi, Martin Luther King: in other words, Charismatic Leaders of the Breakthrough of God. To be in the cadre of the Jesus Movement of our time—that is my Calling.

KAIROS

My Calling is to be like Jesus in the kairos. KAIROS in New Testament Greek means "time." Not chronos, chronological, clock and calendar, one-damn-thing-after-another "time." Kairos is the time, the moment, the right time. It means that everything is in the timing.

The Jesus Movement, says the Gospel, came "in the fullness of kairos." I learned it in the Civil Rights Uprising. We had a century-old system that an entire race wanted changed for decades. It had often been unsuccessfully sabotaged, but was passionately supported by a majority entrenched with money, law and tradition. It was challenged in the kairos by a small minority conditioned by centuries of servility, terror and un-education, was, without precedent, brought down like the Jericho wall, a tide in human affairs, taken at the flood, leading to world-shaking fortune, the time of God's coming with power.

It is obvious that my Calling is to be overturned by whatever kairos comes along. I have friends who've spent professional lives devoted to one cause, shepherded time and energy keeping focus on the one thing they felt called to do. Most of them accomplished more than I, but that isn't my Calling. I'm the kairos-guy; my life a line of dominoes toppling from cause to cause in its time, then moving on. I'm embarrassed about it.

I've never had what Jesus called "eyes to see, ears to hear" the kairos when it's come. It has never come to me from among my people. It's been the marginalized wretched of the earth who got it, and I've never been wretched or marginalized. It's all seemed chaotic, disruptive, senseless and blasphemous to me—until those wretched and marginalized came for me and knocked me off my head onto my feet. That's my Calling, to be somehow marked, for whatever wretched and marginalized, in whatever kairos, to come and get me.

PROPHETIC

THE PROPHETIC is the Kairos proclaimed in corrupted ordinary chronos, the Charisma of the Breakthrough of God embodied in a scandalous presence, the Eschaton of destiny lived right out as if such a thing were really possible. It is the unlawful truth spoken in the face of entrenched, reactionary power, the bearing of Charisma among powerful majorities who have no ears to hear, no eyes to see so outrageous a thing. It is the untimely reminder, insisted on ad nauseam, that the meaning of History is not this unjust present, that God's surely coming future sits in radical judgment on it. It is uncompromising, aimed not at workable solutions but ultimate destinies. The Prophetic Calling is hell to pay, says Jeremiah, but says in another mood, the sweetest life to live.

The Prophets were ordinary humans propelled by the Kairos into a singular charismatic role. This, in the outworking of History, got them published in the Bible with universal archetypal significance. Amos, the original prophet, was "not a prophet," he insisted, "but a herdsman and pincher of sycamores." It somehow got in him to join a luxurious procession to the big religious festival at Beth-El. There, in the fabulous ritual celebration, he had the foundational Prophetic Charismatic experience. And God was in it. His outburst so staggered conventional religion that it could not be forgotten, not then, not at the time of Jesus, not in the moment of Dr. King, not now. I'm not called to be Amos or get my book in Scripture, any more than to be messianic, crucified or raised from the dead. It's just to speak, in its moment, whatever truth nobody wants to hear. It's something I almost never do. But I've done it, and know the feeling—and the consequences. It's my Calling.

ESCHATOLOGICAL

ESCHATON is the surely coming Kairos. Living eschatologically, "The Way" of Jesus, lives toward the coming Kairos, when the hoped-for impossible has its time. Every Kairos has a prehistory. Jesus' Movement thrived because Prophets lived toward it, tried and failed the mission, left tracks. At the Kairos Jesus was ready because he knew the Prophets. Had Gandhi or King tried what they did any earlier, like so many before them, they'd have failed. But had others not tried and failed, the Great Ones wouldn't likely have attempted their revolutions, or, had they, wouldn't have succeeded. Their predecessors lived eschatologically in "The Way." Despite reality they lived as though it could be done. In fact, it couldn't, or couldn't yet, but they kept truth alive in face of false reality. They laid tracks for the Glory Train coming someday, and built bridges, with their slain bodies, over the chasm of hopelessness toward the right time.

If Cliff were still with us, he would hawk this memoir: "Brought to you by the Book of Revelation, the bloodiest, most violent, second-sexiest book in the Bible. Your old-fashioned, faint-of-heart have their Matthew, Mark and Luke. But for zip in your life, blood-tingling terror, some fun… Revelation's your book." Revelation teaches me about eschatological living, My Calling.

I'd be different but for Revelation, and it prods me to be still more different. I admit to liking its creepy images and violence. Carol is judgmental about the "trash" novels I read. I have a sliver of guilt about it. Like me, Revelation's author got carried away with Religious Evil. But I understand the first Christians who loved Revelation. They were fed to lions for God's sake, mad as hell, vindictive. But beneath the vindictiveness and violence is empowering certainty of God's surely coming future. The Empire will be crushed to rubble; the Jesus Movement's Kingdom of God is true parable of our destiny. Whatever movement catches us up makes necessary contribution to that day. The Prophets' Calling, and Jesus' Calling, was to live, not according to the realities, but toward that day, consequences be damned. I don't live that way. But once or twice, in the prophetic moment, I have. And I knew at that moment it was My Calling, too.

EKKLESIA

EKKLESIA is Greek for the Jesus Movement after Jesus. Disastrously, it came to be translated "Church," and Church came to be the corrupted institution of Christendom, the reduction and undoing of the Jesus Movement.

Me and Cliff had fun with Pentecost, the explosive beginning of Ekklesia, Jesus dead, the cadre in the "upper room" desperate, mourning their calamity of existential disappointment. Then in a rush, it came on all of them, at once. Jesus' moment was over, but IT wasn't over. They were on fire, literally, swept up in a human conflagration, exploding into the chaos of mid-eastern streets. They were talking revolutionary jargon over-spilling mere human tongues like true believers I've met. Their specific talk the rabble couldn't understand (just as I couldn't all those times), but what essentially they were saying, the people got (as I did): the new world coming, embodied that moment in themselves.

Then one of the New Testament's two or three comic lines, the best Cliff found in the whole Bible. Someone asked what these guys were on. "They're not drunk," one said, "it's but the third hour." I still hear Cliff bellow, "It's not happy hour yet!" Kairos overwhelmed them, moved them in true-believer enthusiasm to cash their holdings into the common pot ("original communism," said Engels, Marx and Kautsky), in and out of jail, upending the order, living life as it should be, as in their manifest hope it surely will be. Rulers were enraged, as if they really might "overcome someday." They were, says Scripture, Ekklesia.

The Ekklesia story focuses on Saul, brilliant young Turk, thick Turkish accent, a reactionary religious fanatic, a Pharisee enraged at the Jesus Uprising. Saul was a bystander outside Woolworth's screaming at me and Skeet, a prune-faced parent in Student Movement days, or one of my disfellowshipping colleagues in Ohio. But more fatefully, Saul became me. Blindsided, traumatically converted by the Jesus Movement, he got his name changed.

"Paul," they called him, a new handle, transformation of more than mere moniker. I never liked Paul, and get off on documenting ways I'm different from him. But truth is, Paul's me. I was like him when he was Saul and like what he was later. Like him I was religiously one thing, and became, radically, another. Like him I found identity by first rejecting the Movement, then found it in great stories of Scripture. Like Paul I'm a newcomer to the Breakthrough of God Movements of my time. I'm outsider to the cadre, a former enemy just in from the other side, struggling with the jargon, never entirely getting it. Like Paul, who unlike me spent his youth in serious scholarship, but who, in the end, became an activist, I finally went with what I had and got on with it.

Paul got a lot wrong. I blame him and "pseudo-Paul" authors of Pauline epistles for turning Ekklesia into "Church," but I'm probably wrong. One of his heresies I actually appreciate: of Church, he said, "We are the Body of Christ," meaning, Church is extension of the Incarnation through the alleged "Body and Blood of Christ" in Communion. I believe that not of the Church, but of Ekklesia. In its Moment, Ekklesia is incarnation of God and embodies God in its passion for Justice. God "hears the cry" of the people and "comes down" into it. Movements that upended me were the incarnation of God, not their out-workings and routinizations, but their breakthrough moments. We are—in the moment of Kairos, in the power of its Charisma—the Body of Christ, the Breakthrough of God. Having been sucked into them, movements are My Calling.

Authentic Church

Although "church" is a perverted translation of Ekklesia, I suffer the Calling to do church anyway, as if it really mattered. Religion is inevitable. It is, in more or less every culture. There's bad religion, God knows, but there's clearly authentic religion really reaching from here toward God. My Calling is to do religion, but do it (whatever this means) right.

Some of my highs have come in movement churches: Dexter Avenue Baptist, Montgomery; Sixteenth Street Baptist, Birmingham; First Baptist Capitol Hill, Nashville; Ebenezer at the first Martin Luther King National Holiday, 1985; Warsaw Cathedral in Solidarity's uprising; a Lutheran church, East Berlin, the year before the Wall fell, mimeographing dissident tracts that led to its fall; a Russian Orthodox house church, forty people crammed in to worship, plot strategies and care for fugitive members; Esperanza Baptist, facing the heavily armed Presidential Palace in San Salvador, operating illicit missions of social change, its members among "the disappeared"; First Baptist Managua, Thursday afternoons waiting for Gus Parajon (number one on the Contra hit list) to return through assassination threats from weekly medical missions; Latin American base communities, seeds of profound life, a major chapter when Church History of the last century is written; in Myanmar, Brang Sang and his revolutionaries, serving communion to them on their battle maps, AK47's ringing our circle; Tokyo Peace Church. These churches, for a time, were engaging and interpreting the Breakthrough of God, what the Bible calls "prophetic remnant," bearing authentic witness.

AUTHENTIC CHURCH is to prepare for the coming Breakthrough of God, and, when it comes, to embrace and interpret it. Inauthentically, Church has sacramentalized the Breakthrough of God in the Jesus Movement, as if it were the only one. Any manifestation of God, the Church implies, must be exactly like that. In fact, it happens all the time and is never exactly like that. Hence, inauthentic Church inevitably opposes the Breakthrough of God.

I know God least in church, and most in the streets when change is "blowin' in the wind." But I've known God still more with my church in the streets, and wouldn't know God at all except for a church interpreting, saying God was in it. When the Breakthrough of God comes, a church either embraces and interprets, or in its religious function, opposes it. To embrace it, to claim that the wild disturbance of an uprising is the Breakthrough of God, is all risk, pure Faith. There's no certainty to it.

But when the Breakthrough of God is upon us, embracing and interpreting it is all a church can do. Between the times of breakthrough the church's authentic role, say the Gospels, is "prepare" and "be ready." Incarnation comes when least expected. Pastoral care, preaching, and liturgy, are social function opiates of the people unless it's done eschatologically, pointing toward the coming Breakthrough of God.

Koinonia Farm in Americus, Georgia, was two decades in the belly of segregation, an eschatological island living toward the day when the races could live productively together, with no discernible chance that day would ever come. I, however, can testify that when my life was blown off its foundation by the Breakthrough of God in Montgomery, a few miles to the west, I got my bearings because of Koinonia. It bore witness that what we began to dream had been going on in South Georgia for twenty years. To prepare for the Breakthrough of God is to stand with the wretched of the earth, waiting for God. It's among the wretched of the earth that God will surely come someday.

CHARISMA

CHARISMA was Greek for the leadership of Ekklesia, two millennia before Weber made social science and politics made a tactic of it. Charismatics in the Kairos of Pentecost got a "gift"— from God. It first appeared "as tongues of flame" on their heads. Then it was "tongues," speech, penetrating the chaos of languages, crossed purposes and incompatible interests that had undone the mythical Tower of Babel and made true speech and community impossible.

Charisma then fell on all in the Ekklesia, different Charismata for each one, enabling the revolutionary community to be transformative. Charisma is the Breakthrough of God in the Kairos, in movement leadership. Charismatics lead the people "who have ears to hear and eyes to see" that the Kairos is upon them. More importantly, it embodies the people.

Leaders receive from the Breakthrough of God the symbols and ritual that communicate God to them. All we knew of Charisma until Weber reduced it to social science is a short essay in First Corinthians. It's the two-sided building block of Ekklesia, "Calling from God" on one side, "Gift of God" on the other. Everyone in Ekklesia has it: a Calling to be in it, take the risk, serve a particular function, and the requisite Gift of power to pull it off. It's the radiance and force of the Kairos erupting in the voice of each member. My Calling is my Charisma, which embodies its attendant Gift.

I learned this watching my children acquire theirs and make family of us. Carol's is the glue, among many other things, a charismatic wife, mother, and now grandmother. Chris was born with hers, the unfailing ability to light a room and the gifts of a compassionate therapist. She and Peter later acquired Charisma for deep and lasting friendships. Peter got Charisma for enflaming a classroom, awakening knowledge and enthusiasm from students.

Dan was slowest to talk, out-shouted by siblings and when

he did talk, was quiet. He stuttered awhile, an instinctive tactic to hold the floor, but one day he got voice and began to argue. Making enjoyable argument became his gift to the family. He even argued with Kitty ("Mudda," the kids called her) who brooked no argument. No one else argued with Mudda. Once, taking us to an upscale restaurant, she instructed him to don a jacket over his T-shirt. "Why?" he calmly asked. "It's polite," she said, obvious. "What's polite about it?" he asked, incredulous. "It's thoughtful. Others wear jackets." "I don't care what they wear, why should they care ..." and on it went. Peter and Chris were frantic for him to shut up until Mudda was in tears, Danny in his T-shirt comforting her. In time he got a fierce wit and the best ability among us to write and politically strategize. He got the Charisma of skepticism, as for instance, to the more sentimental of his dad's enthusiasms. It came, as from nothing.

Mine includes silliness with children, being a dog-person and having dog-friends (the human companions to my dog's friends). It's discerning others' Charisma, calling it out, going with the moment, taking risks with impossible causes. It's being outrageous as a tactic, finding and injecting humor in unfunny situations (weddings, funerals, boring meetings, tense counseling sessions, deathbeds). And to confront the world barefoot. I actually wear shoes, but scores of friends claim they've never seen me shod. Once, at a peace conference in Sweden where I had leadership, I sat regularly barefoot in a covey of Russians in black shoes and black suits, even when they marched off daily with bamboo fishing poles for a morning's sport. At another conference I discovered Nicaraguans were sharing their meager resources to buy me shoes.

My Charisma is also my "Gift." For instance, I regularly get away with proverbial murder. My kids say I have a cat's multiple lives, regularly surviving near-fatal falls and colossal mistakes. I was once arrested at the Philadelphia Airport as a terrorist. I flew in for a day-long meeting and walked to the airport venue, taking a road running in its direction, but the road ended at a chain-link fence. I could see my destination beyond an overgrown field and concrete roadway. So I crawled under the fence and through the grass, and was crossing the roadway brushing brambles off my suit. Suddenly I saw police vehicles roaring my way. They fanned round me, screeched to a halt, gorged forth cops with guns and riot gear who slammed me down, frisked me, lifted my wallet, pitched me into a paddy wagon and whisked me to airport security where I saw my criminal statistic lettered across videos. Interrogation revealed I'd been on a runway, apparently to wreak terror. Ultimately cleared, I was carted by official vehicle to my meeting—in time to give the devotional.

My Charisma is also the Gift of having Carol there, the necessary one among the other "Gifts." Carol is the wise one in our partnership, the empathetic perspective one, the careful one, who has My Calling at heart and is my fiercest defender, but who is appalled at about half my shenanigans. I think I said this a couple of times already.

My experience of Charisma, getting the momentary Calling in the Kairos, being momentarily filled with "the Gift," finding my very own peculiar voice welling up my throat is exemplified by two bizarre moments. One was the Vassar "Amazing Grace" event. The other was the peace mission in Baghdad, three weeks before the first Gulf War.

I had the wad of Granville children's pictures to give Iraqi kids. We were at a monumental public space for a televised ceremony. A thousand children in military uniforms, boys in brown, girls in blue, lined opposite sidelines of the plaza, four ranks facing each other. We stood at one end of the ranks before an Unknown Soldier altar awaiting our wreath. The children chanted, "Yes! Yes! Saddam! No! No! Bush!" East side answered the west. In English. For us!

They were joyous, engaging with pure innocence the world-political hullabaloo, great brown eyes sparkling, their high-pitched chant a song. I was overcome by them. Without thought, I ducked under the yellow tape and strode the dozen feet to their line to take hands of four on our end, half a thousand more stretching a hundred yards beyond. On auto-pilot, I moved down the column, taking hands, registering brown eyes, pointing at myself, saying, "George." "Farook!" A beaming boy stopped chanting, hands reaching. "Amira!" from a blue-clad girl from the back, tumbling over the boys. "Zaha!" said another girl. Down the line the chanting trailed off, giving way to a chorus of names in rhythmic answer to my "George!"

I thought of the pictures of the children of my church stuffing my pockets. Mark Robertson's toothy grin came out, into the hands of Saleh who leapt up and down. That was the end of the chant, as blue girls plunged on brown boys, shouting, "Picture! Picture!" Children surrounded me, kids from the west side thundering the fifty yards to mob from behind.

Here came a huge Iraqi man, AK47 armed, a soldier sure enough. It struck me where I was, ruining a nationally televised ceremony on enemy sacred ground. Through the kids he plowed, bent over, ear to the mouth of a tiny girl, lifted her and said, "This Sohreh. She want picture!" She got Marie Jaquish. I was out of pictures, shrugging shoulders.

A girl, showing off her English, shouted to American me (I kid you not), "I love you!"

"I LOVE YOU!" I cried back, crying for real. Now that was the chant: "I love you!" the song of a thousand children, and "I LOVE YOU!" from the Amazing Grace guy.

Three weeks later in my Ohio living room, gasping through tears and puddles of tragedy, I watched the bombing of Baghdad, the beginning of the end of the old order. Romeo and Juliet we'd been, smitten in the charismatic upsurge of love, Montagues and Capulets of hate poised, murderous, all around. And there it was: the rockets' red glare, the bombs bursting in air, proof through the night of the unthinkable loosed on the world. Its likely not many of those children survived that death-night, or death-embargo of the ensuing decade, or death-ravages of the first and second Gulf Wars. I harbor a fantasy that Sohreh, thirty-something, has on a wall of her room the curled and faded snapshot of a toothy Ohio kid.

In the end, My Calling is to know myself—in the Socratic sense. It's to unearth my innate answers to life's existential questions, to be myself in the existentialist sense, to do, to accomplish my Destiny. I'm called to know my Sin belabored above. It's to know, embrace, love and join the work of my Ekklesia, the uprising community that bears the Breakthrough of God in my time. It is to seize the Kairos in my Chronos, acknowledge, with gratitude, my Charisma, and live it. It is to know, to be, to accomplish my Theology. "My Theology," no bundle of doctrines, is rather the profoundest aspect of knowing myself.

I am, like you, in the words of the second Creation myth, "in the image of God." This is the terrific insight—compelling, but drawn back from—at the base of Hindu and Buddhist revelation. It is "That of God" in Quaker silence, the extravagance in Walt Whitman's poem, that he (unwashed, bearded, profane) is God! To know my theology is to sink into my image, also God's, and imagine from there. Or, as my friend and theologian Tom Driver said in *Patterns of Grace*, "All my experience is Word of God for me." And My Calling.

One more thing.

THE NEAR-ONES

Jesus said it's the Sh'ma, to Love God with all I am and do, and my neighbor, THE NEAR-ONES, the ones in my face, as myself. What I've said so far is the "Love God" part, God, the Worldly One encountered in the Breakthrough of God on the road, in the present Kairos. I'm called to join "my heart, soul, mind and strength" to that, but that's not the end of it. I thought it was. For far too long I imagined My Calling to "love neighbor as myself" the neighbor being the other cadre, the masses of our solidarity encountered there. I wasted a lot of time perfecting myself thusly, nearly missing the one thing needful.

It turns out the "neighbor," the near-one I'm called to love as myself is not a movement, colleague or victim of injustice. Them too. That's not what the Sh'ma is about. The near-one, the one who's in my face, is Carol. It's Peter and Patrick, Dan and Jen, Chris and Joe. It used to be Kitty and Daddy, Nanny, Bobby Reddy—all gone now, no longer in reach. Also Bertha and John D. Wagster, Carol's beloved parents, parents of John, Richard and Wanny, who with their spouses, Lynda, Suzie and Ashley, their children and grandchildren, became genuine family for this only child. And Cliff. And Mac. Nowadays it's cousins, nieces and nephews, best friends. And Nicholas, Caroline, Riley and Theo, my fabulous grandchildren. The near-ones whom I am to love as myself.

Like Peter and Paul, my name was changed in earthquake encounters, on the road with God. Defining and treasured actual names I got from these near-ones: "Jawidge" from Kitty, "Dahlin'" from Nanny, "Butch" and "Butch-o," and Carol's secret name when we fell in love. Peter named me "Daddy," Dan "Dad," Chris (I kid you not) "Ding-a-ling," and later, when she learned French, "Ding-Soir." Nicholas pronounced me "Gin Gin," and Caroline took it up. Riley, exposed to plenty of "Gin Gin," said I was really "Baba," as in her world I am. Theo has gone with Riley. It is, first and last, My Calling from God to be a good husband, a good dad, good granddad, and good friend. If I'm not that, whatever else I may seem to be is hypocrisy, one I've indulged plenty.

It's something my daughter Chris told me from her son Nicholas when he was four. She and Joe put him in "Zoo Camp," a week at the Central Park Zoo. When she asked what he learned on the first day, he proudly replied, "Mammals." "Oh? What about mammals?" "They have hair!" he informed with authority. "Really?" she said uncertainly, thinking whales, dolphins, etc. "Did you learn that different things are mammals? Even people?" Nicholas screwed up his little face, trying to give Mom some benefit of the doubt. But no, he couldn't go that far. "Well," he offered gently, "Gin Gin doesn't have any hair. Gin Gin's not a mammal."

Ain't it the truth.

AUTHOR'S NOTE

The reader may have noticed a peculiar use of capitalizations throughout the book: words like, "Civil Rights Movement," "Sit-in," "Black Activists," "Student Movement," "Students," "Women," "Gay Activists," "LGBTQ Uprising," etc. I've deliberately delayed explanation, in hopes that your curiosity has been pricked. Having now brought up this "Breakthrough of God" business, it's time to come clean about it. The capitalized words turn out to be catechism in my quirky theology. I understand God in terms of the Breakthrough of God as I've encountered it over the time of my life. The capitalized words represent the moments (i.e., "Sit-in") and the people (i.e., "Blacks") who bore the Breakthrough of God in my experience. They are therefore theological words, in my bizarre vocabulary, and deserve capitalization.